MY LIFE

in the

MAINE

WOODS

A GAME WARDEN'S WIFE IN THE ALLAGASH COUNTRY

MY LIFE
in the
MAINE
WOODS

A GAME WARDEN'S WIFE IN THE ALLAGASH COUNTRY

ANNETTE JACKSON

ISLANDPORT PRESS

ISLANDPORT PRESS

Islandport Press
P.O. Box 10
Yarmouth, Maine 04096
www.islandportpress.com
info@islandportpress.com

First Islandport Edition: July 2007
Latest Islandport Printing: May 2023
Printed in the United States of America.

Original edition published in 1954 by
W. W. Norton & Company, Inc.

ISBN: 978-0-976323-19-8
Library of Congress Card Number: 2007929672

Dean L. Lunt | Editor-in-chief, Publisher
Teresa Lagrange | Book Designer
Emily Lunt | Book Designer

To Those I Love Most

My husband, and my four children,
Arlene, Robert, Hilda, and David

Editor's Note

Our 2007 edition of Annette Jackson's *My Life in the Maine Woods* is different in many ways from the original—in many better ways, we hope. When reissuing an out-of-print book there is always some tension between keeping the book identical to the original or changing it in ways that we believe will improve it. Part of this is easy; we always try to add photographs and flesh out the author's life story, and sometimes we add new material that reflects the importance or relevance of the work. For example, that is the approach we took with our reissue of Helen Hamlin's classic, *Nine Mile Bridge*. Making the decision to go beyond that is a little more difficult, but fortunately for us, we did not make the decision alone—Annette did. A decade or so after her book was published, Annette went through and revised her original text, adding some details here, deleting some there. It was that revised text that we received from her daughter, Arlene Packard, in 2005. We edited the book to better integrate the revisions. Arlene also submitted to us a second book written by her mother that was a collection both of columns originally appearing in the *St. John Valley Times,* and original unpublished writing. We decided to use some of that material to enhance *My Life in the Maine Woods.* In fact, one entire chapter from that second book is now part of the new *My Life* (the last chapter, "Thirty-Two Years Later: Back to the River").

While this is not the typical process for "reissuing" a book, in this case we think it is in keeping with what Annette wanted to see happen, and we believe it makes this book an excellent and improved version of Annette's wonderful tales from the North Woods. We hope you think so, too.

Dean Lunt and Amy Canfield

Contents

Annette Jackson

Make no mistake: Annette Jackson loved the Maine woods. Loved nearly everything about them. She fished, hunted, canoed, hiked, and accompanied her husband—none other than famed game warden David Jackson—on many of his official travels. Throughout the Allagash region, Annette took full advantage of the gifts the Maine Woods offered, all while keeping house and raising children.

"I was determined not to be just a game warden's wife," she wrote. "I wanted to learn to follow old trails, paddle a canoe, fish, shoot a rifle, hunt, and above all, snowshoe. I wanted to be a partner to my husband in his work. This meant that I would have to be ready on a minute's notice to accompany him. I soon learned to have my housework up to the minute and to have a few cookies always in the cookie jar. If I baked beans I would double the amount in order to put some in sealers to steam and preserve for storage. I put up other kinds of food in that way: meat, fish, vegetables, soup, and even Boston brown bread. These could be kept for days and would be ready for us when we returned home late and had to get a meal in a hurry."

Annette Hetu was born July 28, 1906, to mill-working parents in Massachusetts. Her mother, Emma Pelletier, was from St-Pamphile, Quebec, Canada, a small town just across the border from Maine. Like many girls in the late 1800s, Emma left home to work in the textile mills in Massachusetts. There she met Joseph Hetu: they married, and had their first child, a daughter, Mary. Ten years later, Annette was born, but then, just months later, her father died. Emma's family back in Canada encouraged her to return home with her two daughters, and she did. As a child, Annette spoke only French, and learned to read

Photo courtesy of Arlene Packard

Annette Jackson, 1950s.

and write English before she learned to speak it fluently.

When Annette was about seven years old, her mother married Julian Caron, a man who proved a kind and loving stepfather to Annette through the years. Annette was also close to her younger half-brother, Lionel.

The Carons moved across the border to Seven Islands, a large farming settlement on the upper St. John River that later would host a huge lumbering operation. Annette's stepfather ran a successful farm there and was also the postman, delivering mail to the farmers, lumber camps, wardens, and others throughout the area. During the winter he trapped, and all in all, he provided a good income for his new family.

At the time, there was no school in the area, so Annette was sent from the ages of six to ten back to Canada to a "teacherage," a home where she boarded with a teacher and received basic education. When Lionel also reached school age, the Carons decided that both he and Annette needed a better education than a teacherage could provide. They sent Annette to the St. Louis Convent School in Fort Kent, and Lionel to a school connected to what was then called the Madawaska Training School. Each fall, the children boarded a train and made the hours-long trip to school, not returning home to Seven Islands until classes were over in the spring. Annette and Lionel spent each Sunday together while away at school.

Annette left the convent school after the eighth grade, ending her formal education. But Annette loved to read, a passion she carried into her adult life and one that kept her company on many a dark, cold night when her husband was out on patrol.

"She told me how she used to put a towel under her door so her mother wouldn't see the kerosene lamp burning late into the night so she could read," Arlene Packard said.

She also educated herself in outdoor sportsmanship, learning the secrets of the woods from the outdoorsmen she lived among.

"As a teen she hunted and fished. Where they lived it was what you did. She always did," said Packard.

When Annette's mother became ill, the Carons moved from their farm to Lac Frontiere, a small town on the Maine side of the Canadian

Photo courtesy of Arlene Packard

David Jackson in his game warden uniform.

The Jackson family, 1930s. (L to R)
Annette, Arlene, Dave and Hilda.

border that was also a crossing station; a swinging gate separated the two countries. Annette nursed her mother and kept house for Lionel and her stepfather. It was difficult, but Annette lived in her dreams, her daughter said.

Annette met Dave Jackson by chance. Out with her family in 1930, the Carons came upon a motorist who was out of gas. It was Dave, the new game warden at Umsaskis Lake south of Seven Islands in the Allagash Wilderness area.

"Through our dusty windshield I got my first look at the new game warden, and through that same dusty windshield, at first sight, I fell in love," Annette wrote.

Dave Jackson was born on a farm on the banks of the St. John River on September 2, 1902, the eldest of David Jackson's and Elizabeth Gardner Jackson's six children. His father was a lumberman and farmer. When his father bought a farm in Allagash Plantation, he moved with his family to the large house with a barn and a number of outbuildings, situated near the meeting point of the St. John and the Allagash rivers. When his father died at age fifty-six, Dave inherited the farm, which he would hold on to for decades.

In school, Dave had a gift for arithmetic. "He could add up long columns of numbers in a matter of minutes," remembers Packard. Like his future wife, Dave, too, finished school after the eighth grade. As a young man, he left home for a job as a surveyor for International Paper Company, mapping uncharted territory in Canada.

In 1929, he became a game warden, and was assigned to Umsaskis Lake, his first assignment in what would prove to be a long, successful and legendary career.

"He was just a good, honest and loyal man," remembered Packard. "When help was needed anywhere on the St. John River, he was the one that was called upon to help."

In her classic book, *Nine Mile Bridge*, Helen Hamlin writes of David Jackson: "He knows that country as well as he does the palm of his hand. He has cruised the woods all his life, and he is the best canoeman in the state of Maine. My hat goes off to Dave when I hear the often repeated tales of his running Devil's Elbow on a spring freshet, or how he bluffed two backwoods Canadian poachers into dis-arming when they had the drop on him and were hold-ing him off with a rifle."

Two years after Annette first laid eyes on Dave through that dusty wind-shield, they married. The small wedding ceremony was held in Jackman on Easter Sunday, 1932. A few days later, the newlyweds were off

Photo courtesy of Arlene Jackson

Sportswoman Annette Jackson (left) with a buck shot near camp on Big Black river.

to Umsaskis Lake, to the remote warden's camp that would be their home.

Their honeymoon was brief. Dave soon left to inspect lumbering camps and stayed out for several weeks. Annette went right to work, too, making curtains and adding other feminine touches to what had been Dave's bachelor quarters for two years. And she quickly adapted to being alone at the cabin on the lake in the woods.

"It was not easy to learn how to break up the monotony of the day at first. But when you are young, healthy and strong and in love with your husband and the wilderness, life does not seem monotonous. Life, as the old saying goes, 'is what you make it.' You may make it sad, or you may make it exciting and good—I chose exciting and good," she wrote of those early days.

Her book is a testament to that decision.

Her love for the wilderness quickly grew. Neither black flies nor bears, bone-chilling cold nor blizzards prevented her from availing herself of nature's wonders throughout the seasons. She grew close to far-flung neighbors, from hermits and trappers to fire wardens and lumbermen. She shot her first buck. She learned to cook venison and partridge, and her specialty was cooking over a campfire. These are the many and varied experiences she recounts so powerfully in *My Life in the Maine Woods*.

"My mother was a person who saw someplace and began to think how to make the best of the situation, and she did love the challenge," Packard said. "That was her way of belonging to an area—she saw it as an opportunity."

Annette and Dave had three children while living at Umsaskis Lake. Arlene was born in 1932. Robert was born in 1933, and Hilda in 1934. Annette, who had no previous experience with infants, quickly learned the joys and duties of motherhood, but she didn't let her new role prevent her from getting outside and enjoying fishing and hiking.

"She used to carry me around in a basket," Packard said.

Later, she'd bundle the children up and entertain them with dogsled rides on snowy winter days.

"Our home was always made very comfortable," Packard says. "She was great with a sewing machine, learned to grow a great garden and canned all the vegetables we had for the winter months. She had busy hands; she was always knitting someone a pair of mittens. She was a reader and a writer; I can still hear the tapping of her typewriter in the early morning hours. She was recording her memories."

In 1938, Dave was promoted to chief of the Allagash district. The new position required the family to move about forty miles to Allagash Plantation, which the Jacksons agreed would be beneficial for the children, especially since Arlene was now school age. But it was a bittersweet decision for Annette.

"It was with an ache in my heart that I began packing

Photo courtesy of Arlene Jackson

Arlene, Annette and Dave Jackson.

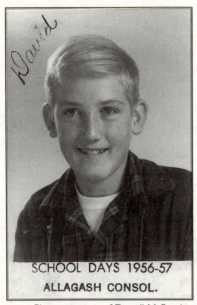

SCHOOL DAYS 1956-57
ALLAGASH CONSOL.

Photo courtesy of Darrell McBreairty
David Jackson Jr.

for our move. I hated to bid good-bye to that part of the timberland and to all those beautiful lakes. Now that I looked back on them, my years in that part of the wilderness were all too short. They were time enchanted, just as all the forests and lakes thereabouts were enchanted places," she recalls in her book.

Annette and Dave had their fourth child, David, in 1944. In time, Annette took an active part in town affairs and served on the school board. But her greatest joy during those "town days" was heading off into the wilderness again with Dave on his many trips. It was during this time that she started writing *My Life in the Maine Woods*, which was first published in 1954. In the 1960s, she also wrote a popular column, "The Wisdom of the Timberlands," for the *St. John Valley Times* newspaper.

By this time, the three older Jackson children were well on their way to their own lives. Arlene was working as a teacher. Robert was looking to a stint in the U.S. Army. Hilda would marry her hometown sweetheart, an Air Force man, and move with him to Eglin Air Force Base at Fort Walton Beach, Florida. Little David dreamed of being a game warden himself one day.

Dave retired in 1952. A few years later, he and Annette decided to spend a winter near Hilda and her husband in Florida. They thoroughly enjoyed themselves.

"Fort Walton Beach in those early years was very primitive; the only thing there was the Air Force base," remembers Packard. "They still hunted there and fished. Mother loved the beach, and they'd always have picnics there."

The Jacksons decided to make the winter trip an annual event, and eventually bought a small house in a wooded area of the beach town. They'd head south each year after hunting season, and return to Allagash Plantation in the spring. Young David made the trips, too, until he was older and decided to remain in Allagash.

Sadly, after being hospitalized for depression, he committed suicide in 1964.

Photo courtesy of Arlene Packard

Three of the Jackson children in 1999 (L to R): Arlene, Robert and Hilda. It was the first time they were together in 40 years. Their brother, David Jr., died in 1964.

"My mother grieved each day for that loss," said Packard.

It was painful, so that year, with what Annette described as "a dark cloud" hanging over them, Annette and Dave decided to winter again up north in the wilderness. Annette took over as postmistress at Clayton Lake, and Dave took a job as a scaler with a lumber company. "They said, 'It's available, let's do it,' " Packard said. It was, perhaps, some type of closure.

The next winter, however, they returned to Florida.

In 1971, Annette was diagnosed with cancer. Dave made one more trip back to Maine to sell their Allagash properties. When he returned to the Sunshine State, they were both in Florida for good.

Annette died in 1971 at the age of sixty-five. Dave died in 1978 at seventy-five. Both are buried in Fort Walton Beach, where Hilda still lives, along with Arlene, a retired teacher and widow. Four of Annette and Dave's six grandchildren live there as well. Hilda has four children and Arlene has a son. Robert, who joined the U.S. Air Force, married, and lived in Idaho, died in 2000. He had one daughter.

Arlene, who remembers being so proud of her mother when *My Life in the Maine Woods* was first released, is even more proud to see it being reissued today.

"It is my wish for her," she says. "She had real adventures. I'm so glad she did."

Foreword

by Cathie Pelletier

If you stand today in the woods of northern Maine, or along the riverbanks, and listen for a few quiet moments, you will hear whispers. Skeptics might say it's just wind sifting through the trees. It was pine, after all, that lured the first settlers here nearly two centuries ago, hardy men and women who came to cut timber for the King's ships. It *could* be the wind, but I prefer to think that the whispers are voices. They are the voices of all those people who lived years ago, who fell in love, who raised families, who knew laughter and heartache, and who are now disappeared forever.

Sometimes, in those same woods, and along those same riverbanks where fiddleheads and wild shore onions grow, you might hear a soft fiddle music, ghostly and faint. Again, the doubters will say it's just a tree leaning like a bow across another and moved by that same invisible wind. But it always sounds like a real fiddler to me. After all, these woods have known a lot of old-time Saturday night dances.

The names that fill our oral history in Allagash are the names of loggers, river bosses, big lumber company barons, brawlers, game wardens and the best damn storytellers this side of the Mississippi River. Woods work was a man's job, and back then, in that time and place, it was a man's world. But here and there among the stories of burly men are mention of a few women who knew what life was like in the Maine woods when lumber was king and isolation a way of life.

Annette Jackson's name is one of them.

Reading her book, as well as *Nine Mile Bridge* by Helen Hamlin (another of those female names that survive in our oral history), I cannot help but feel an intense sadness for a way of life that has gone. I know well most of the place names that Annette Jackson mentions: Umsaskis Lake, Fall Brook Lake, Musquacook, Churchill Lake, the St. John River. I was born and raised on the banks of the St. John. I even knew some of the people she writes about in this book. Mealy Mullin, for instance, was a lively and strong lady and many townspeople today remember her fondly. The Bill Pelkey who brought Annette in his canoe down to the house where she would give birth to her first child is my great-uncle. (Pelletier became Anglicized into "Pelkey.")

And I knew Annette Jackson. When I was still very young she came to my home a few times and visited with my mother. In her later years, long after she left the Maine woods behind, she wrote a column for our local newspaper, *The St. John Valley Times*. A photo of her appeared each week above her column. An aspiring writer even then, I was so impressed that someone we actually knew *personally* was in the paper each week.

While I don't remember ever meeting Dave Jackson, he also visited my parents in our home. What I know of him is what my father once said: "If Davie Jackson told you something, you could believe it."

Annette Jackson and her husband, Dave, were a part of my town's life, of its history and its evolution. They knew how to survive in snowy woods when the temperature dropped to forty below, and that wasn't considering wind chill. They knew how to hunt, and fish with flies they made by hand, and to grow big gardens. They knew how to find entertainment by sitting on a cabin's front porch as a red sun dropped into the lake, or beyond the tops of all those thick pines and spruce and fir. They knew how to make ice cream from snow, and furniture from discarded wooden boxes. The radio was to that time period what the most impressive home movie theater is today. But even if a radio would work so deep in the woods, the music they loved most came from the throats of birds, the slap of a beaver's tail on water, the splash of a fish, and wind beating rain across the roof of their cabin.

This way of life is gone now, as are Annette and Dave Jackson.

If the novelist Thomas Wolfe is right, that we "can't go home again," then the next best thing is to pick up a book such as *My Life in the Maine Woods.* It's a testament that pays homage to a past that exists only in faded photographs, and in modern oral history that must compete now with television, cell phones, computers and the Internet. This book is the door to a museum, one that opens onto a wilderness that still holds the ghostly sounds of loggers filing past to their work camp, of steam log haulers, of a single ax against virgin pine, of stories told at night around a red-hot woodstove in some tiny cabin on the shores of a dark and wind-blown lake.

When Annette Jackson herself left the deep woods, left behind the way of life she writes about, and came to live in our town of Allagash, she wrote these words: *Forty-five minutes later we landed in the middle of the St. John River, about half a mile from the house I was to live in. With our three children, a suitcase, and a bundle of blankets, I stood on the shore for a few minutes not knowing which way to go. I looked up over the high, snow-rimmed banks of the river that I would have to climb. Suddenly I noticed two boys on top of the bank. Out of curiosity they had come to see why the plane had landed. I waved to them, making signs for them to come to my rescue. With much hardship we climbed the steep, slippery bank of the river, carrying the children who were then beginning to feel the cold of an early spring day. We hiked across*

three hundred yards of open field to the main highway and thence
down a quarter of a mile of paved road to our new home.

To write this foreword, I drove up to the Allagash bridge
and stood there for a few minutes looking down at the hill
Annette climbed that day with her children, sixty-nine years
ago. My grandfather, Tom Pelletier, would have been running
the ferryboat that crossed the river at that spot, years before the
bridge was built. This is the point where the Allagash flows north
to hit the St. John. Grampie's house, where my father was born
and raised, is now gone. But the old Jackson homestead is still
there, lived in now by another family. As I stood on the Allagash
bridge, I tried to imagine the scene Annette described, the river
still locked with winter ice, the banks steep and slippery. I imag-
ined her bringing her children safely along the shore and up over
the hill to what would be her new home. That was such a long
time ago. And yet, as I stood there remembering, I heard the
faint whisper of voices. I heard a ghostly music on the wind.

Cathie Pelletier
May 4, 2006
Allagash, Maine

Cathie Pelletier is an Allagash native and author. Her books
include *Running the Bulls*, *A Marriage Made at Woodstock* and
The Funeral Makers.

She has also written *Candles on Bay Street* and *Dancing at the
Harvest Moon* under the pen name K. C. McKinnon.

Chapter 1
Game Warden Wife

In the summer of 1930, as we returned from a weekend visit to an old aunt who lived along the St. Lawrence, my mother, father and I came upon a stalled car about five miles from Lac Frontiere, near the border between Quebec and Maine. It was two o'clock in the morning. My father stopped our car, got out, and went to see if the driver needed help. When he returned, he informed us that the man in the car was Dave Jackson, the new game warden at Umsaskis Lake.

"Apparently he doesn't know that gasoline stations are far apart in this section of the country," my father said. "I'll see if I can draw enough gas from our car to get him to town."

Through our dusty windshield I got my first look at the new game warden, and through that same dusty windshield, at first sight, I fell in love.

Two years later, we married.

Reverend David Jones blessed our marriage on a beautiful Easter Sunday in Jackman. We were met there by Dot Shelley, an old friend of mine from Seven Islands, on the upper St. John River. (Dot was the person who taught me to speak English.) Her husband, Randell, another game warden, was also there. After the wedding Dave and I returned to Lac Frontiere, which was where I had lived after Seven Islands. Then, after a day there with my family, we left Canada and headed for Umsaskis Lake, in northeastern Maine, where Dave was stationed. As I sat at his side on the ride to the camp, my thoughts were fixed on the new life I was to live. It was a sunny morning after two days of stormy weather. It had snowed, a light rain had fallen, and on

1

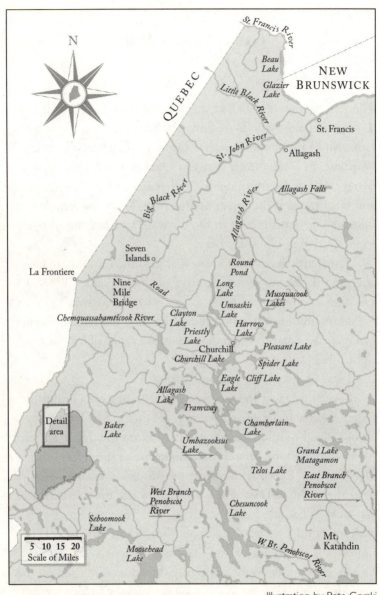

Illustration by Pete Gorski

Northwestern Maine

this clear frosty morning the trees glistened like diamonds. The road seemed like a dark streak through the snow, barely wide enough for the car.

We drove to Clayton Lake and stopped at the post office. There we met our friends, Dot and Ray Burnham. Dot came from Michigan, and at one time she had made the same kind of trip to a new home in the wilderness.

"Well, Ray," my husband said, "I've got myself a cook, too. I should eat pretty well from now on."

We had a short, pleasant visit but had to hurry along, for we had several more miles to go and a lot of work to do after we reached Umsaskis Lake. The game warden's camp that Dave occupied sat a quarter of a mile from the main road. You could reach it by automobile in the summer, but you were forced to snowshoe in during the winter.

When we got to the mouth of the road, a pack, two pair of snowshoes, and some packages were taken out of the car, which was then put under cover. My husband handed me the smaller pair of snowshoes and loaded the rest of the things on his back. In my excitement I had not thought of the walk in to the cabin. Under a fancy pair of overshoes, I wore shoes with three-inch spike heels. While I was in the car nothing had been required of me, but on snowshoes I was a sight. As we began our trip I stumbled at every other step, and I could see Dave looking back with a grin on his face. I was well aware that he was having a good time at my expense, and I thought to myself that had I been in his shoes I would be laughing out loud. I kept straining my eyes looking for the cabin. I finally saw it at the base of a little hill, but how I came down to it I will never know. All I do know is that I felt two strong arms helping me and then I was sitting in a two-room cabin. It was small, but cozy and very clean.

"This will do us for a while," my husband said. "As soon as I have some free time and can get Tom Sweeney to help me, we'll build a bigger, nicer one back of the hill and down the lake shore a bit. Meantime, we can make do here all right, can't we?"

We certainly could.

Umsaskis Lake is three miles long and slightly less than a mile across at its widest point. Our camp was built in 1913 on the north shore where there had once been a large clearing and another camp. Our 15-by-17-foot home was originally built as a children's playhouse, but it was big enough for us. It was built just a few feet from the edge of the water. When we looked out from a hillside facing a large ledge on the other side of the lake, we had a view over the entire lake. There are several camping grounds on the shores of the lake. Glazier Brook flows into Umsaskis opposite Pine Point, where huge pines shade a beautiful camping ground and keep the springwater nice and cold all through the warm season. Umsaskis lies in the course of the Allagash River. Starting at the foot of Churchill Lake, the Allagash proper runs through rapids a few miles before it enters Umsaskis. From there it flows to Long Lake and on downstream through Round Pond until it reaches Allagash Falls and down to the mouth more than fifty miles below Umsaskis where it empties into the St. John River.

But this is by no means the whole extent of the Allagash watershed. Above Churchill Lake there is a series of lakes—Eagle, Chamberlain, and Telos—all of them connected by waterways that the woodsmen call thoroughfares. In addition, a lot of smaller lakes and streams feed into this chain. Thus from Chamberlain, Allagash Stream leads up into Allagash Lake

A young Annette Jackson, probably in the 1930s, around the time she married David Jackson.

and Mud Pond Stream into Mud Pond. There are also the Leadbetter Ponds and Ellis or Bog Brook. Around Eagle Lake lie Indian Pond, Pillsbury Pond, Haymock Lake, and a regular web of small streams—Snare Brook, Russell Brook, Soper Brook, Smith Brook, and Woodman Brook. Churchill, the last of the chain, has Cliff Lake, Spider Lake, and Pleasant Lake, together with Thoroughfare Brook, North Twin and South Twin Brooks, and Churchill Brook. Finally, the Allagash River is fed from the east by Harrow Lake and the Musquacook Lakes—First, Second, Third, and Fourth—and from the west by Priestly Lake and Chemquasabamticook, together with many streams and brooks too numerous to mention.

After only a few days together at the camp, Dave left to make his regular inspections of area lumber operations. A game warden has no exact hours nor any special schedule.

His district was large, including about twenty townships, some fifty lumber camps, and three thousand men scattered through the woods, since at that time lumbering was booming. Game wardens in those days did not have the use of planes. The only means of travel were by foot or canoe in summer and by snowshoe in winter. There was little travel by car. During a spell of weather in the spring or fall, my husband could be home much more, but during the summer, patrol duty—checking fishermen on the lakes and streams—was done by canoe. Night patrol, too, was necessary.

Although this trip was to last several weeks—and I was going to be alone—I was told not to worry and to keep my chin up. Still, as I stood at the cabin door watching my husband move across the lake, I sensed for the first time the feeling of being alone in the wilderness. I had often wondered what people did while living in the wilderness; now I had the opportunity to learn, as I was all on my own.

I entered the cabin and sat on the edge of a chair to survey the two rooms I would call home. As bachelor's quarters they looked pleasant enough, but with a woman around something had to be added. The rooms were severe and lacked any feminine touches. After several hours of planning I looked over the things I had brought with me.

I thought our bed, which was covered with a tan arctic sleeping bag, looked dreary and cold. Although the bag had cost quite a bit, I would slipcover it with a bright spread. It took me some time to choose between a light green or a yellow fabric. I finally decided on green and added a rose-colored cushion. In the opposite corner of the room was a round-topped table fashioned out of a tree stump. I covered it with a white-and-blue-checkered tablecloth, and put a fancy little candy dish in the center. On the night table beside the head of the bed I placed our portable radio, and near it the desk.

The small windows presented a problem. I wondered what I could possibly do to make them appear larger. Rummaging again through the things I had brought, I shoved aside some dish towels that I would need when I got around to arranging the kitchen and smiled when I came across five yards of white percale with a small blue pattern. Long ago there had been a sale at one of the stores back at Lac Frontiere, and I had bought the material to make myself some aprons. Instead, when I got it home I put it in my hope chest for later use. How glad I was now to have it to decorate my windows, and how pleased I was to find that it would match the tablecloth!

By this time it was late, so after a quick supper by lamplight, I settled down with a book. Later, with the earphones of the portable radio pressed tightly against my head, I tried to locate a program. But after an hour, I gave up. There were so many switches and buttons it was impossible to get anything. I must admit that I was somewhat timorous about the prospect of my first night alone in the wilderness. It was midnight before I finally fell asleep, and throughout the night I awoke with a jump at the least little noise.

The next morning my neighbor, Mrs. Bartlett, who lived two miles away, phoned and invited me to visit her later on in the day, saying that she would send Maurice, her husband, for me. I thanked her heartily but explained that I was very busy making changes in the household and it would be a few days before I could go to see her. I promised to call her and asked her to call me again.

After Mrs. Bartlett rang off I went back to my curtains, which I had to sew by hand. It took quite a while, but by twilight I had put up the last one. The room didn't look the same; its atmosphere was thoroughly changed. One thing that helped was that I had enough curtain material left for a skirt around the sideboard which stood by the stove.

The second evening I found much longer than the first. At dusk, just as I was going to light the lamp, I noticed a dark shadow not far from the front door. I tiptoed to the window and found myself face to face with a big doe. I was strangely relieved to find that she was as surprised to see me as I was to see her. The next evening I put some food out to keep her coming. It was nice to have someone around—even an animal.

On the third day I looked for a small piece of birch to make a towel rack to put over the basin. The cabin by this time was

Photo courtesy of Arlene Packard

David and Annette Jackson.

pretty well redecorated and I was proud of the work I had done, knowing that my husband would enjoy seeing it. The ruffle I had put on the shelf behind the cookstove added a pretty splotch of color to the brown logs which partitioned the two rooms.

The remaining days until Dave's return were the longest in my life. But despite heavy spring winds and rain, I managed to take a walk every day, following several old trails. I soon adopted the habit of hiking up a trail leading to the ridge. I needed fresh air, and these walks broke the monotony. Furthermore, from the ridge it was fun to look down on the lake and watch the ice get thinner and thinner and then blue as the days slowly became warmer.

I was determined not to be just a game warden's wife. I wanted to learn to follow old trails, paddle a canoe, fish, shoot a rifle, hunt, and above all, snowshoe. I wanted to be a partner to my husband in his work. This meant that I would have to be ready on a minute's notice to accompany him. I soon learned to have my housework up to the minute and to have a few cookies always in the cookie jar. If I baked beans I would double the amount in order to put some in sealers to steam and preserve for storage. I put up other kinds of food in that way: meat, fish, vegetables, soup, and even Boston brown bread. These could be kept for days and would be ready for us when we returned home late and had to get a meal in a hurry.

If one will preserve different kinds of food in the manner in which I just described, he will get along nicely in the woods. Especially toward midwinter and early spring when vegetables and fruits are not available, it will be an appetizer for your meal, not forgetting that it is good for one's health.

One of the things the woodsmen never have is fresh fruit, with the exception of dried fruits, stewed or made into pies. They seldom see an apple, never oranges or grapes or bananas. The craving for sweets is another experience far worse than the lack of vegetables or fruits for the woodsman. In the lumber camps of long ago, the only sweets available were a little molasses, which was used to sweeten tea. As for the woodsman who lunched in the woods, molasses was carried in a bottle and added when lunch was served.

When good weather came later on in the spring, I was able to enjoy many canoe trips with my husband. Although there were lots of camping grounds around the lakes, there was nothing I liked better than to watch Dave select a site just for us. He would paddle along the shore comparing the different spots and finally select one from which he could command a view over the entire section he was to watch. I loved those places where the ground was covered with a soft carpet of moss, the trees thick overhead, the area open enough so that we could put up a tent, build a fireplace, and set up a small table.

We always pitched camp early enough so I could get in at least an hour of fishing. Then we would have our supper of fried trout. Nothing tastes better than trout fresh from the water. Boughs make wonderful beds, and once they are properly arranged on the ground they are as soft as a feather mattress.

On our way home from our first spring trip, we found a nice patch of fiddlehead ferns and picked enough for our dinner. These, Dave said, would be very good for they were young and tender. You boil them with a little salt and a piece of salt pork the way you cook other kinds of greens, and serve them with a few drops of vinegar.

I often watched my husband from the bow of our canoe and I took great pleasure in watching him paddle or use a set pole, which is rather difficult, because with it comes a large amount of power and push to take you up the stream or up a river. The set pole can be used on the left or right side of a canoe. It is made of straight grain wood about ten and a half feet long, weighing two pounds, this depending on how large the canoe is. It will vary in size depending on the canoeman's choice.

In later years, we often carried our canoe on top of the car when my husband had to make a check on Churchill Lake or Eagle Lake. If we did not do this we would have to go up through the Chase Carry, below the dam at the foot of Churchill Lake. Chase Carry is a narrow strip of dangerous rock-strewn water about one mile long; it was named after the first man to settle at Churchill Lake. There the white water flows so fast that it is impossible for anyone to follow the channel. I have seen very

11

David Jackson with his sled dog team.

few woodsmen who would undertake to go up it, although every summer fishing parties making the famous Allagash trip come down through it. A good many of them smash their canoes and lose their equipment.

The first summer I was at Umsaskis Lake one party came through and lost everything they had taken with them, including their canoe, which was broken in two. One of the party walked the remaining mile to our camp. I'll never forget how the man looked. He was covered with blood. His face, arms, and chest had a swarm of black flies on them. He asked if Dave would come to where the rest of his party was, to help them recover some of their lost belongings. Dave said that he would go, but before doing so he cleaned the fly bites, washing them with disinfected water and swabbing them liberally with camphorated oil to help heal the sore spots.

A game warden in this part of the wilderness has more than just the job of game warden. Many people come to him with their troubles. He looks for lost persons, searches for drownings, fights forest fires, and gives first aid.

Chapter 2
Neighbors

Although we lived in the wilderness, we did have some neighbors. Down through a mile-long thoroughfare lay Long Lake and at its foot was the dam where Ed Taylor lived. The dam holds the water for the purpose of driving lumber. Ed's work as keeper was for days just to sit back and see that the dam was not tampered with. Then he would get an order to raise the gates for more water. Ed had traveled much in his young days. He had been on a transport ship that delivered goods to all the important seaports of the world. He spoke often of his crossing the Amazon River and dipping up a pail of water from it. He was a big man and did not look his age. He had blue eyes, and his complexion indicated that he must have had light brown hair, perhaps blond, when he was young.

Ed had lived almost his whole life in the woods and at the age of seventy-five had been hired to look after this dam. He lived in a two-room house miles from anyone. When people came to see him he didn't have much to say. He treasured his privacy so much that he had his visitors sleep in a little camp about fifty feet back of his house.

Ed would get up very early in the morning, and the first thing he did each day was to walk over to the calendar, and with a large nail he kept for the purpose, punch a hole through the date, but always a day ahead. Somehow he had convinced himself that in this way he would never be wrong. As for the time of day, he went by the sun. "When the sun does not shine, what do you do then, Ed?" I asked him one day. He only grinned.

He never listened to the radio, never read a newspaper, but still, he knew most of what went on. He kept his house nice and clean, but he never made any improvements inside or out. I used to praise him for the way he kept his dish towels snowy white. And he could make the best molasses cake!

Whenever I think of Ed Taylor I recall Tom Sweeney, another old-timer in these parts of the woods. Each spring Tom was hired to go to Long Lake Dam to help Ed. The first few days would go along well, but then Tom would start a batch of yeast bread and Ed would start a pot of baked beans and both would want the oven. The beans would win, so Tom would be moved into the guest camp for the rest of the spring.

Tom was a handy old woodsman. At the age of seventy he was still able to travel on snowshoes and look after his trap lines. He had lost one eye, and his face was out of shape on one side so he had difficulty in holding his pipe, which he smoked continuously. He was six feet tall and had a wonderful head of hair. I remember a lot of people asking him how he kept it so thick and black. He said he massaged his scalp with kerosene oil and then brushed his hair vigorously. He loved to cook and he always promised to show me how to bake biscuits. I was not very successful with biscuits in those early days. Dave could bake them well, but to get him to do so was a problem. He said he had cooked for himself long enough.

I remember that before my first canoe trip, Tom presented me with a very light paddle—all smooth and varnished. That was the one I learned to paddle with. Dave had painted on it a picture of one of the big trout he had caught at the mouth of Gray Brook.

Eventually, Tom became our nearest neighbor. In a clearing about a quarter of a mile right above our camp, where the land sloped downward toward the lake, he repaired an old lumber camp and moved in. His cabin was set back near the edge of the woods, and he used the front part of the clearing for a garden. When the St. John Lumber Company had operated in this area many years before, the clearing had been the landing place for logs, and the little camp Tom had repaired had been the scaler's camp. Tom was a woodsman from way back. He had held assorted jobs in the woods and had worked as blacksmith, cook, walking boss, and many others. Now he had taken to trapping. He loved Umsaskis Lake and never wanted to live anywhere else. Although he had three married children, he refused to live with any of them.

One evening when we were sitting around the campfire and Tom Sweeney was puffing away at his pipe that he loves so well, he began to tell us of the old days. His stories seemed unbelievable but they had actually happened. In the days he told of, men didn't seem to mind walking a distance of seventy-five or eighty miles. Once, he said, he left Umsaskis bright and early in the morning and through sixteen inches of snow made his way to Chemquasabamticook Stream. There he stopped at the lumber camp and had lunch. Then he continued on to the mouth of the Allagash where he had a snack and rested a few minutes. Thereafter he kept going until he reached Connors, where he was to board the train which was to take him into Fort Kent where his family resided. All this distance, seventy-three miles, he covered in one night and one day.

I asked Tom how many times a year he would go home. He told us that usually he came into the woods early in the fall and went back in the spring. A good many of the other woodsmen would wait until the lumber drive and follow it through to Bangor.

If you followed the shore of Umsaskis to a cove above our camp and Tom Sweeney's, you would come to the Bartletts' camp. Maurice was employed by the Forestry Department as a chief fire warden. Like ourselves, the Bartletts were very fond of the wilderness. Back of the Bartletts' camp is Priestly Mountain and then Priestly Lake. The lake lies southwest of Umsaskis Lake and its water flows into Priestly Brook and on through Drake Brook into Umsaskis. This little stream has been a source of satisfaction to many fishermen, with wonderful catches of trout weighing three and a half to four pounds.

South of Umsaskis Lake lived the Louis Pacquet family—Maman, Papa, and ten boys and girls. For many years the Pacquets hired a private teacher for their children. One of the children was named Camille. One day Camille, who was about ten years old, took some matches and went into the shed where the wood for the winter and some empty gasoline drums were kept. Camille wanted to see the inside of one of the drums. He struck a match and poked it into a hole near the bottom of one of them. No sooner had he done this than he hit the roof, his face and hair all burnt. The cover of the drum went through the roof making a big, jagged hole.

Maman Pacquet was terrified. She came running out of her house just as Camille was trying to get up. After looking him over, she decided that the only thing to do was to rush him to the doctor who lived sixty miles away. She wrapped him up, put him on a hand sled, and pulled him over the two miles to our camp. Luckily Dave was home. He took poor Camille to the doctor's and fortunately, after a few weeks, the little boy was well again.

From May until October each year Louis Pacquet worked as a fire warden, and the rest of the time he was a scaler. This latter work took him to lumber camps where, whether timber was being cut for long logs or pulp, it had to be measured. The long

logs, which are usually fifteen to twenty feet long, are scaled—
that is, measured—for length and diameter, whereas pulp is measured by the cord. A cord is a pile of wood eight feet long, four
feet wide, and four feet high. The scaler keeps the amounts in a
small book, and every night his report is given to a clerk at the
office. In order to indicate who has done the cutting, whether of
logs or pulp, a sketch mark is made on the ends of the sticks, and
in that fashion each individual can be paid accordingly. These
days men are paid so much a foot or cord, but many years ago
they were paid by the day, and it is said that in 1900 they got
as low as twenty-five cents a day. These jobs open up as soon
as lumbering begins in the fall, and they last until spring. The
jobber is an individual who agrees to cut so many feet of lumber
or so many cord of pulp in a given length of time. He will move
to a camp of his own with perhaps fifty or more men, depending
upon the amount the company has given him to cut. Then he
employs his own scaler, just as the landowner has his.

Above the Pacquets, in a little camp about two hundred
feet away, lived Gus Tarr. "Oncle Gus," as everyone called
him, had gone twenty-one years without seeing the outside
world. However, he was an ardent reader and had no trouble
keeping up with the news and changes of the times. He lived
with his niece, Myrt, and they had a very happy and harmonic
living arrangement. Oncle Gus had been a game warden here
in 1906, but for many years now he had trapped and also was
with the Forestry Department stationed at the Priestly Tower
during the summer months, about two miles from our cabin at
Priestly Lake.

Every day when Oncle Gus went to the tower, Myrt would
go with him. The tower was thirty-five feet tall, and from its
top on a clear day you can see for miles around. On one of our
visits to Oncle Gus, Dave took me up the tower. At first I was

somewhat alarmed, but Dave warned me not to look down after we had gone halfway up. I felt strangely insecure, as if the wind were making a special effort to blow me away and would succeed at any moment. But I got over that feeling and enjoyed the view without fear of the height. Seeing the outlines of the lakes and streams and the beauty of the wilderness from way up was an unforgettable experience for me. I saw the figures of fishermen miles and miles off and in spots, the deer feeding on the shores. The fire warden's tower, which rises above the tall spruce forest, is so near the lake that when you are inside it you have the impression that you can reach out of the window and wash your hands in the blue water.

In order to see Oncle Gus and Myrt at the camp outside of the tower, we had to choose a rainy day. Oncle Gus would meet us at the landing with his boat and outboard motor and we would sail across the lake to his camp. Priestly Lake during the summer months spells enchantment. The lake itself is very small with several brooks and springs emptying into it. Fishing is excellent throughout the fishing season. Because of the deposit of several thousands of small salmon many years previous, it is nothing to cast and hook a good-sized one. The lake is set in the center of a heavy growth of spruce with an odd silver birch here and there. The elevation surrounding it is high, and trees lower over the water's edge, leaving very little of the shore in sight. Being the guest of Oncle Gus and Myrt was always something to remember and well worth getting out in the rain for.

We often walked around Priestly Lake. At one spot overlooking the lake you come upon a carpet of soft pale-green moss with specks of gray in it. Here the trees are thick and shady and there is always a breeze from the water. I liked to sit in this spot and watch fish jump out of the water for flies, or a deer coming to drink at the mouth of the brook. Frequently you could hear the loons call and see wild ducks flying overhead.

Back at Umsaskis Lake, on the same side as Oncle Gus's cabin, southwest about half a mile, is the Lacroix Company's depot. It is situated in a cove at a point where the lake is at its widest. A depot is a large set of buildings including a boarding-house for the men, a cook room, a storehouse for the food, and a barn (or hovel, as the woodsmen call it) for the horses. This depot is large enough to accommodate a couple of hundred men at work. In back of the depot is a road that going south heads out over a ridge which makes the divide between Glazier Brook and the Musquacook Lakes region. This road runs on out to Ashland.

The head of Umsaskis Lake extends very wide and is partly filled with dri-ki, the woodsman's name for dead trunks of timber that have been killed by the flow of water backed up by a dam. Upstream the Allagash is barely wide enough in low water for a canoe. Then as you reach Chase Carry it widens to a quarter of a mile and soon the water flows in white foam over sharp rocks all the way up to Churchill Lake Dam. Many years ago when the lumber companies were driving square timber logs, this dam backed the water up into Eagle Lake and from there into Chamberlain Lake through Lock Dam. Then the lumber could be floated from Churchill Lake through Eagle and Chamberlain into Telos, and then through a short canal which had been dug at the head of Telos down finally into the East Branch of the Penobscot and on to Bangor. This changed the course of the upper Allagash waters from north to south.

When my husband was out on patrol he usually followed the shore, taking in the many brooks that flowed down from the surrounding lakes and camping grounds. All this added up to many miles each day if one had to cover Churchill and its surrounding lakes and the four Musquacook Lakes, Clear Lake above them, and Harrow Lake which flows down through Harrow Brook into the Allagash River at the foot of Chase Carry. Then near Churchill there were lakes to patrol: Little and Big Pleasant Lakes and Spider Lake to the east, and Cliff Lake to the south, all of which feed into Churchill. Trails and tote roads enabled Dave to follow the brooks and patrol all these lakes, taking in at the same time the cuttings, the lunch grounds, and the lumber camps. Churchill Lake itself is three and a half miles long and three miles wide.

The land in this region I would call rolling country with no large mountains in view. While traveling through the places I have mentioned, one finds the forest, after a large cutting, bare. One sees only a mass of treetops down over some underbrush in among some very small spruce and pine that are left because they are too small to be of use. Once this "slash" (as it is called) dries, it is very dangerous and likely to be the source of forest fires.

Leaving the upper end of Churchill Lake one passes through a thoroughfare a mile long and enters a round pond which is a half-mile wide and a mile long. On either side the land makes up into ridges which divide brooks and lakes. By the shore it is low land until you come out on Eagle Lake. Then Soper Mountain makes its appearance over the treetops to the south of Eagle, and one is able to distinguish the fire warden's high tower on the peak. Dave's work took him to all the brooks and coves where camping grounds were usually built. Russell Brook on the west side of Eagle Lake was a favorite with many. So also were Smith Brook, which leads up into Haymock Lake, and Woodman

Cove on the other side of the lake. Then there is Pillsbury Island, which is the most beautiful of all. Here one has to be smart and arrive before someone else has pitched camp, for almost everyone who is acquainted with Eagle Lake will rush for that place.

On the west side of Eagle Lake was the camp of another game warden—Bert Duty. Above Bert's camp is the Tramway and Lock Dam leading up to Chamberlain Lake. The lake was not in our district and therefore we always turned back at that point. Besides, every time I had a look at it, it was so terribly rough I wouldn't have wanted to venture out in a canoe. Farther to the west lies Allagash Mountain. From the west shore of Chamberlain on an up-and-down trail one can go by rail, on a hand car, through the forest over to Umbazooksus Lake, which lies to the west of Chamberlain Lake. From there Mount Katahdin can be plainly seen.

Chapter 3

My First River Trip

I n July, my husband was due to make a trip to Tramway for
a checkup on several camps, brooks, and lakes, and I was to
go along. This was to be my first trip to Tramway, which is on
the west shore of Eagle Lake, and one bright summer morning
almost before I was fully aware of it we were on our way, with
food for five days. The canoe was loaded on top of the car which
would take us over the ten or more miles from our camp on
Umsaskis Lake to Churchill Lake.

It was a beautiful day, very hot, but with a breeze and a very
clear sky. It was that kind of day that we so seldom see. The
breeze we felt on our faces would make it an unforgettable day as
we glided over the smooth surface of the water.

As we drove along the road through Churchill to the boardinghouse,* little children peeped out from doors and windows to
look at us. The few mothers I had already met walked to their
doors to wish us a cheerful "Good morning." They were clad in
clean white starched aprons, and from our car we could see the
shiny black stoves trimmed with bright nickel in the kitchens
behind them.

My husband told me they had a large schoolroom which
seated twenty-five or more pupils and that we would visit it some
time in the near future. A young girl talking French only and
preparing the children for their First Holy Communion could
be heard in one of the rooms upstairs in the old boardinghouse
building. This boardinghouse was about one hundred feet long

---

* In *Nine Mile Bridge*, Helen Hamlin describes in detail life at
Churchill Depot in the 1930s, where she spent a year teaching school.

and forty feet wide. I think it must have had a hundred windows and doors. As we went by, the aroma of coffee filled the air. Enough had to be made for nearly one hundred lumbermen.

We continued on, crossing the dam and passing by the storehouse and a blacksmith shop and garage. It was about nine o'clock in the morning when we arrived at the wharf on Churchill Lake. Three parties of fishermen who were on their way up the lakes were already there. As usual, my husband spoke to them, asked them where they were going, and checked their licenses. While this was going on I wandered along the shore daydreaming as I looked out over this immense, beautiful body of water.

Then suddenly Dave made a loud whistle like a deer and I returned to the wharf. The canoe was already loaded heavily, and I was told that if we were to have fried trout for dinner we had better hustle. Dinner time was not far off.

When we came to Cliff Brook, as it was called, Dave remarked that this was one of the best places in the area to fish. Using a small buck-tail fly, I made my first cast. I got all tangled up in my line. Then, to top everything, I got the line caught in the bushes behind me. My husband was very patient with me, for he knew I was trying my best to become a good sportswoman. One thing I admire especially in him is that he never ridicules.

I finally landed my first one, a beauty which weighed about half a pound, and Dave said, "Hey there, you get too many of those and fishing is done for you today."

I didn't know what to do—you couldn't be choosy, you had to take them as they came. So I said, "This one is all I want for my dinner. I'll let you fish for yours."

I passed him my fishing rod. I thought I had given him enough trouble, what with getting me untangled and having to climb a tree to save the line and hook which had gotten caught.

Part of the fun of fishing is finding a place by a nice little brook, and cooking the fish right after they are taken from the water. That is when they are most tasty. I was elected to cook on all our trips, so it was up to me to learn any practical way of making a meal as delicious as I could. After all the years I have spent in the woods, I can get a meal ready as quickly on an out-of-door fireplace as I can on a gas stove. My husband always provided the fireplace, and got the best kindling wood that could be had.

Don't ever try frying trout in butter on an outdoor fire. The best thing to use is salt pork. You put a few thin slices of it in your frying pan, hold the pan over a not-too-hot fire, and keep turning the slices over and over until they are nice and brown on both sides. Then you remove the slices and keep the remaining fat to put your trout in. You slash the trout once or twice to keep them from curling in the hot fat. Keep turning them over. Trout fresh from the water are difficult to cook but they are delicious fried this way.

Tea is something else I learned to make on an outdoor fire. Place the amount of water you need in a kettle with a bail on it and set it on the fire to boil. When the water is boiling, put in a teaspoon of tea for each cup and take the kettle off the fire. Just before serving, add a little cold water. This makes the tea leaves sink to the bottom and the tea very clear in color.

Then there is johnnycake. This is nothing more than cornmeal cake, but a State of Maine woodsman always calls it johnnycake. You make it with a cup of white flour, a cup of cornmeal, a little sugar and salt, one egg, two cups of milk, and two teaspoons of baking powder. First you mix the dry ingredients, then add the liquid and mix it all well. Finally you pour the batter in a greased pan and bake it baker-style in front of the campfire. When it is cooked golden brown, johnnycake is the most tasty of all bread and a sure way to any woodsman's heart.

Most trappers and guides bake cakes before an open fire out of doors in this fashion. They use a baker made of sheet metal which stands on four short legs and is sometimes called a reflector baker and often a Yankee baker. It is open on one side where the pan is inserted and this side faces the flames. In this way the cake receives heat that is both direct and also reflected from the metal sides of the baker, on top, from the back, from the bottom, and from the sides. It is just like a small tin lean-to with a shelf in it facing the fire. If I had my choice and the money to do it, I would spend three seasons of the year following the rivers, brooks, and lakes and baking shortcake baker-style.

As we continued on our trip Dave stopped here and there to check the many fishermen along the way. Finally we arrived at Camp Parsons, on the north shore of Churchill Lake. Bert Duty had been living there for a good many years. It was dusk and I did not see the outside of Bert's camp too well. But the interior was fascinating. We were welcomed by twenty or more pictures of actresses which were pasted on the wall. I liked the place the minute I got inside. It was a three-room cabin with the larger room in the center and a bedroom on each side. We carried our belongings in and prepared to spend the night there. Arriving late in camp or perhaps to the tenting ground, getting supper ready is not as difficult as it might sound, especially when you both know what you want to eat and you happen to have some fresh trout, and you can eat trout three times a day. As soon as we know where we are to spend the night, Dave built a fire, and while he carried in the luggage and made ready for the night, I started supper. Once an old guide told me a quick way to cook trout, especially for supper. With potatoes which are sliced very thin, put in layers of some pork fat and trout, ending with a layer of potatoes on top, a little salt and pepper to taste, and a small amount of water. Cook this slowly over the fire, and just before serving I add a little canned milk and let the mixture simmer just a few minutes. It makes a most delicious supper.

The next day before we left I had a final look at Bert's place. It was beautiful. The cabin was built on level ground and the front yard was covered with pebbles. To my amazement I also discovered a little house high up in one of the trees surrounding Bert's cabin. Four big birches had grown together making a perfect frame to build a house on. The house, which looked to me like a huge birdhouse, was ten by ten with a slanting roof and one window. A ladder from the ground enabled one to go up and down readily. I asked Dave what Bert kept in it and he suggested that I climb up the ladder and see for myself. So up I clambered. It was very cool up there. One bed and a night table completed the furnishings. Dave informed me that the flies were not so thick up there, and it was always cooler on warm nights than down in the camp. So Bert frequently slept in his treehouse.

The lake was a little choppy as we left, and I asked Dave whether he thought it would get worse. He said that all depended on the wind, but I could see that that was not what he was thinking. Not that I was afraid, but I hadn't liked the big whitecaps I had seen before on Umsaskis Lake, and it seemed to me that Churchill Lake would get even rougher in bad weather since it was much larger than Umsaskis Lake. However, the choppiness got no worse that day.

When we arrived at the Tramway, it was pretty well deserted. Only the caretaker of the Lacroix Company and two fire wardens who were stationed there all through the dry season could be found. The boardinghouse, which stood three hundred feet from the shore, was painted white and looked very inviting. It was a building almost one hundred feet long and about half as wide. The inside was all furnished. It even had hot and cold running water. While all but deserted now, this place had at one time been booming.

I asked my husband where Tramway had gotten its name. He explained to me that when some lumber company began operating in this area, it imported an enormous loop of heavy wire cable which was rigged up so that when properly hitched to a power engine it could be used as an overhead conveyor to haul logs across the height of land lying between Eagle Lake and Chamberlain Lake. In earlier days it had been the custom here to do such hauling with oxen. Now, with the conveyor functioning, miles of carrying and ox driving were averted. Later, in 1924, the Eagle Lake-West Branch Railroad moved timber from Eagle Lake to the West Branch of the Penobscot waters.

The story is told that when the Lacroix Company took over, the lumbermen clearing the area where the boardinghouse was to be built found and chopped up enough ox yokes to heat the boardinghouse throughout the whole of the following winter.

There were many interesting old buildings at Tramway, for lumbering had been going on here for well over a hundred years. I explored the remains of one old place which had been built in the early 1800s. This house had been constructed of square timbers held together by wooden pegs. Not a nail had been used in it. Yet it had stood up against the winds and rains of well over a hundred years and was still in remarkably good condition when I examined it.

Edouard Lacroix, a Frenchman, was quite young when he began operating in this part of the timberland in 1926. For his pulp and log and hardwood cutting he employed at one time more than three thousand men, most of them French-Canadians. His honesty, fairness, and industriousness earned him a wonderful reputation, not only among the men who worked for him but throughout the whole area. He believed in paying his men well, furnishing them with the best of equipment, providing clean, comfortable, and attractive living quarters, and feeding them the way lumbermen like to be fed—with good, big, well-cooked, hearty meals. His clerks and scalers lived in large modern houses which he built for them. The lumbermen lived in the huge white boardinghouse, which he also built.

One of the scalers composed these lines about the king of the timber cuttings:

The Man of the Hour

These lines are composed by a scaler, it seems,
Who is scaling the pulp wood at Thoroughfare Stream,
Where the young and the old and the low and the high
Are singing the praises of Edouard Lacroix.

He sure is some hustler to corral all these means
In order to purchase such costly machines;
His mountains of pulp are a wonderful sight,
And tractors are humming by day and by night.

We next made our way to Lock Dam, and had a look at Chamberlain Lake. By that time we were getting pretty hungry, so we searched for a place to eat. We had dinner on Pillsbury Island in Eagle Lake, one of the most gorgeous camping grounds I know of on the Allagash River. You find nice springwater there.

Through broken-up country we continued on to the Woodsman Cove. It would take a man days to come out of it should he get lost there. There were fishermen to check at almost every camping ground and along all of the brooks. The last party

31

we saw was at Baxter Point, a spacious camping ground named after the first governor of Maine to make the Allagash trip. We camped at the Ziggler camping ground on the east shore of Eagle Lake that night and ate supper in a pine grove by the light of the campfire. It was a moonlit night, and after watching the stars for a while we unrolled our sleeping bags and turned in for the night. Lying on the deep bed of boughs, I went happily to sleep listening to the sounds of the night.

The next morning bright and early we did some deep-water trolling with a hundred yards of trolling line, a sinker, and a large hook baited with a five-inch chub. You let the line out and paddle very slowly. I always call this "provision fishing." It is not much of a sport. But a togue—a lake trout—that weighs ten or twelve pounds will give you quite a fight. I'll never forget the first one I caught. Dave, giving me orders on what to do, sounded like the referee at a boxing match.

Fishing is best done in the morning or in the latter part of the afternoon. It took me a long time to learn all my husband's tricks of baiting a hook and then casting. The difference between the two of us is that I always fish for the fun of it while he fishes when we need food. Many times I have watched my husband baiting with a little piece of chewing gum, the fins of a fish, a butterfly, a small caterpillar, a feather found on the shore—just about anything and everything.

On our return trip we canoed to Churchill's Landing by starlight. The lake was calm—not a ripple on it—and the air was cool.

Chapter 4

Starting a Family

O ur first child, a little girl whom we called Arlene, was born in late August. I had planned to go to Dave's mother's at Allagash Plantation for the birth. We made plans to go by water more than fifty miles down the Allagash River between Umsaskis Lake and Allagash. While I was getting ready to start this long journey, my husband received a telephone call telling him he had to be at Musquacook the next day. This upset our arrangements, but nothing could be done about it. While we were discussing the situation we learned that Bill Pelkey[*], a guide from Allagash, was at the dam. So my husband called and asked him if he could take me down to Allagash. At nine the next morning luggage and canoe chair were arranged in the canoe for the trip. I bade my husband good-bye and we parted, he for the Musquacook region and I for Allagash. I was eight months pregnant.

I guess Bill was a little nervous to have me in his care, for he seemed to hurry with every task. But I was well and my doctor had advised me that I could undertake the long trip. When we left Umsaskis Lake and our cabin, I looked back several times and thought of the wonderful experiences I'd had during my stay in this part of the wilderness. I felt certain I would return—only this time with a small baby.

Umsaskis Lake was a little choppy, and I began to wonder what Long Lake would be like. Dave had assured me that Bill was an expert canoeman and had urged me not to worry. As we

---

[*] Bill Pelkey is Maine author Cathie Pelletier's great-uncle.

went by Gray Brook and Chemquasabamticook, where Long Lake is at its widest, the waves were large and furious. Holding on to the gunwale of the canoe, I watched the waves ahead of me—usually one small one, smooth; the next one much bigger, with a little whitecap on top; followed by a third, large, foamy, and furious. Bill handled the motor and canoe expertly and we were soon at Long Lake Dam.

While my luggage was being carried over, along with the canoe, the motor, and the gas can, Ed Taylor, the damkeeper, welcomed me with a cup of hot tea, a piece of his gingerbread, and some bear stories.

Soon we were on our way again. The water was just right for good outboard motoring and we made good progress. The shores following the Allagash River are lovely, and at several places we saw deer feeding on grassy points. As we went along Bill refueled his motor, never stopping once until we reached the Allagash Falls. There I insisted that I would help carry a few things but Bill simply refused, saying that walking was not too good over the carry and I had better just wait. I had made several trips in this area with my husband, so I did not need to ask how far we were from the settlement. By then I knew the names of all the different brooks and ponds. In the late part of the afternoon we arrived at our destination. While those many miles of water through the wilderness might have seemed terrifying to many women, I enjoyed them.

After two weeks Dave returned from his trip and met me at his mother's. A day later we were blessed with a little girl, and my husband returned to Umsaskis to resume his work, promising to come back in another two weeks to take me home.

Although our baby was very tiny, she was healthy and would sleep for hours at a time. My husband and I had had no experience with children, let alone a newborn infant. Dave came from a large family but had left home when he was very young, and I had been an only child for years before my brother Lionel was born. The family doctor gave us an assortment of medicine we might need, and along with it a book on infant care. We started from there.

In the fall of the year they put the camps in shape for the winter cuttings, and men came by the hundreds for the winter's work. During such days my husband was constantly busy checking on the camps. Many of the men who come into the woods to do lumbering work have little regard for the game laws, and consequently the wardens are kept very much on the go. Some of the lumbermen like to trap in their spare time. They set snares for rabbits and other animals—even deer, in some cases. I found out in later years that on one occasion Dave had walked right into one of those snares. Had he not been quick enough he might have been caught in it and hanged. I always found out about these incidents months after they occurred, but after I heard about them my hair would stand on end for a while.

Late fall brings ice storms which make the going slow and dangerous. Hunters come from everywhere and have to be checked on and in some cases watched over like children. I recall one evening when I went along with the baby while Dave patrolled the road from Umsaskis to Clayton Lake. After we had been out a few hours we thought we would call on Dot and Ray Burnham at Clayton to check on any hunters they might be boarding.

When we arrived Dot was at the phone. She hung up the receiver and said, "No wonder I couldn't get you on the phone. I was calling for you, Dave. One of our hunters hasn't come home, and Ray has gone to look for him."

She told Dave the direction Ray had taken that morning. Although it was dark, Dave left to join in the search while the baby and I stayed with Dot. It was two in the morning when they returned with the hunter. They had found him walking on an old logging road, calling out every once in a while. He had used up all the cartridges he had taken with him and he was exhausted. In the years since then there have been many similar occasions when my husband has had to go out in the black of night to search for lost hunters.

Before the winter had settled Dave usually gave his snowshoes a thorough inspection, since in his work, his snowshoes are his lifesaver. On all his long hikes which take him through the woods on his patrol, I have seen him using the bear-paw type which are not altogether round, but oblong with no tail on them. But he also uses a type of snowshoes which are longer, with a tail on them; that and a permanent harness are the best for his work. The bear-paws for traveling in the woods, and breaking trails, and the others for lakes and rivers. Mine are the narrow type since I follow only trails.

I like the permanent harness the best, since my husband claimed them to be the best. These are a narrow strap, two inches wide and just long enough for proper adjustment, with a long belt lacing, one and a half inches wide, which has been called a thong or *babiche*, which is the French name for such. This is long enough to go under the mainstay of the snowshoe, come up on either side of the toe and through a slit in the strap; it crosses over the instep and then a back hitch, leaving double around the heel and drawing tight; returning to the heel, you tie a permanent knot, so that you can slip your foot quickly in and out without having to buckle a strap every time you put them on. This kind of hitch was called by our old-timers and woodsmen the "squaw hitch."

In the middle of December when hunting was over, Dave and Tom put the finishing touches on our new cabin, which they had started a couple of months before and which we hoped to move into soon. They wound up taking our cabin apart, numbering each log. The cabin was built on a high elevation several hundred feet from the lakeshore, and from our front window we could see the entire lake and part of the thoroughfare below it. The birch trees set close to the camp provided shade and made the setting perfect. The roof of the cabin was made of shingles split by hand from dry, straight-grained cedar. The logs inside were golden in color and a raftered ceiling rose to a peak of mellowed cedar splints. Larger windows were set in, too. Tom and Dave installed a tiny cookstove, some cupboards, and a small sideboard with a wooden sink.

Because the cabin was small, the scarcity of furniture seemed unimportant. The windows were large and we painted the frames around them white. Shades and curtains put a nice finishing touch on the camp. Later we bought one rocking chair which I covered with a bearskin. I insisted on a bed with cedar posts with the bark left on, and a table to match. These and a desk and a radio were the most important items we had. All in all our cabin was as snug and as fit to live in as any you are likely to see in the woods.

We moved in on a clear December day. The snow was deep and the trail over the hill to the game warden's camp was soon tramped down from the moving and the repeated passage of sled runners. To this day I don't know why the stove was the last thing to be moved. Baby Arlene was still very tiny and she lay back at the old camp all bundled up in the rocking chair in front of the stove. On our last trip from the new camp to get the stove and the baby, I found to my horror that she had fallen from the chair and lay facedown on the floor in some ashes that had fallen out of the stove. She was crying and trying to wriggle herself into a different position. I lunged at her, picked her up, and cradled her in my arms until she stopped crying. It was a blessing that the ashes were cold and dead and that she was unhurt.

The first evening everyone helped to cook supper. I volunteered to bake biscuits, for I knew it would please Tom, and I liked to hear him say, "Annette, I'll show you how to bake biscuits some of these days."

One of the things that meant a lot to us was the spring which was situated in the woods just behind the cabin. My husband always had a soft spot in his heart for springs. Locating a spring seems not too difficult when one knows all about the color of certain weeds and mosses it seems it is nature's work to give all indications if you really want to look for one. The spring my husband located when we first moved into our cabin was just across the road, some one hundred feet from the cabin door. But a spring has a way, once discovered, to make its way through someplace. It seems that it was no time before our spring overflowed and began to flow directly by the corner of our cabin and down over the hill.

We had been living in our new cabin for several weeks when one day the Fish and Game plane landed. Levi Dow, the supervisor of my husband's district, walked in.

"Well," he boomed, "quite a setup this is."

Levi, who stood six feet tall and weighed around two hundred pounds, had a loud voice and his laugh could be heard for half a mile.

"Hello, Dave and Annette," he said. "So this is the new baby. What in hell do you feed her, Annette? There's no cows up here."

I reached into the desk and showed him the infant care book and told him we used Eagle Brand milk which proved very good for her.

"Not bad at all," he said, as if he knew all about babies, "not bad at all."

Levi visited with my husband that afternoon and then returned in the evening to Fort Kent where he was stationed.

Chapter 5

A New Year

January is the season of rest, and also the beginning of a new
year. With it come many wondering thoughts of what the
days ahead will bring. It keeps you guessing until you have made
up your mind and say, "Come what may, we will make the best
of it." As for nature, many of the tracks which could be seen on
the ridges and swamp are not to be seen anymore. Because of
the deep snow, many of our small animals are sleeping for the
winter. This sleep is called hibernation, and is quite wonderful.
I have often wished to witness one of these animals just waking
from this long sleep.

When the roads were passable in some parts of the timberland, my husband had to make his usual inspection tour, and I
was able to go along on many trips to lumber camps which could
be reached by auto. We looked forward to those trips together.
Some of the years I lived in the woods we were able to scout the
lakes way into the middle of January. We would drive to Long
Lake Dam, which was ten miles from our cabin, in fifteen minutes, and to Churchill Lake and even Eagle Lake. We even went
on midwinter picnics which we enjoyed so much. I found out
that there were few other women who stayed in the woods with
their husbands for the winter months as I did.

I recall one time when all the men who were working at
Churchill and who had cars arranged an auto race on the lake
when it was frozen over. They all lined up as racers do and at a
signal started forward as fast as they could go. Some of the racers
would get going at a good clip and all at once turn into a spin.
Others would get their wheels spinning so fast that they would

make no progress at all. But in all they would have a good, bois-
terous half-hour or so of sport and go home proud, even though
there was no prize for the winner.

People had been ice fishing at the head of Umsaskis Lake,
a distance of about two miles from our cabin, and I began
wishing I could go fishing, too. However, I couldn't very well
walk a small baby that far on a cold day, or any other day for
that matter. Then one afternoon I saw Dave, with an ax in his
hand, going down to the lakeshore. I began to wonder what he
was going to do. By and by he began chopping a hole in the
ice. When it was done he returned to the cabin and told me
we could fish right in front of our house. He suggested that we
let Tom try the fishing first, and if it proved to be successful I
would have a chance to fish also. The fish hole was close enough
so that I could go there while Arlene was napping.

It turned out to be a very good place, and during sunny
afternoons thereafter I used to fish for a couple of hours. We
later sent for a duck-hunting bag we had seen advertised in the
L.L. Bean catalog. This turned out to be just the right thing in
which to bundle Arlene. It was windproof and very warm, and
on many a sunny afternoon I took Arlene along for a bit of
fresh air. Some afternoons we were all there—Dave, Tom, the
baby, and I. We caught a whitefish once in a while and almost
always togue.

One winter's day when my father was visiting us, Tom asked
me if we could have baked togue for dinner. I was delighted, for
I loved to prepare one for baking. I use a togue of about three
pounds and remove the skin, using a pair of pliers Dave bought
me for that purpose. Then I chop very fine four thin slices of

white bread, a small onion, and one or two sour pickles, adding salt and pepper as needed. I scald the bread and mix it well with the chopped onion and pickles. Then I stuff the fish with this dressing and put it in a baking or roasting pan in the bottom of which I first place a few slices of salt pork. I put a couple more slices of salt pork on top of the fish and bake it slowly for about two hours.

On days that my husband was away on his usual rounds I did not have a great deal to do. I busied myself with sewing and knitting. I did a lot of reading and spent a lot of time listening to our radio, often far into the night. Late in the afternoons I carried wood for the stove and enough water to last me until the next day. I followed this routine every day as regularly as I kept to the baby's schedule for feeding and care. About eleven each morning I would bundle up Arlene in the duck-hunting bag and let her nap on the porch. She always woke up smiling and with rosy cheeks. She was growing like a weed.

I found the nights very long when Dave was away. Often the winter nights were very dark and enlivened with wild storms. If I looked out my window I saw the snow drifting wildly. When I opened the door to look outside, the wind had built the drifting snow closely against the door, to a wall several inches high. And when the wind gathered a new strength, it drifted this wall out in the darkness.

Some nights the moon was so bright that you could almost read by its light, and you can see the surroundings nearly as plain as day. The clouds, as they rushed by over the lake, cast their shadows in great patches and seemed to be dancing in the moonlight. When it is below-zero cold, and the ice is two to three feet thick, it begins to crack and makes such a terrific noise that you will never forget it. The next morning if the snow is not too deep on the lake, you may see how the ice is cracked and follow the crevices from one side to the other.

Some of the nights I have experienced alone were so quiet that the silence was almost unbearable, and I wished that I could hear something outside, if only the bark of a fox.

Worrisome thoughts occur too at night. Much as I have tried to banish them I have often bothered myself, when my husband has been away, with silly and groundless visions of Dave sleeping out cold and wet in the stormy night. I should know better than to fret that way, for after many years in the woods, Dave knows his way around.

After the middle of February, perhaps a bit prematurely, my thoughts start to turn to summer. That particular year I was expecting our second child. However, thrilled as I was, it meant a month away from home and from my husband, and I didn't look forward with much enthusiasm to that part of it. All through those months I kept very active, as I was healthy and strong.

Several times during this winter we visited Oncle Gus and Myrt. With Dave carrying Arlene Indian-fashion on his back, we would snowshoe across the lake. I loved going to see Oncle Gus and Myrt. The camp was large, and Myrt, who had a knack of doing things with very little, had made it seem like a picture out of a decorating magazine. Our visits there were always pleasant. We would arrive at about ten in the morning and the time would be spent with "How-have-you-been?" "My-how-the-baby-is-growing!" and "Are-you-lonesome-while-Dave-is-away?" Meanwhile, Oncle Gus and Dave would be discussing the lumbering and trapping and poachers and beavers. Then Myrt would get dinner. She was a wonderful cook and everything was always delicious. After the dishes were cleared away we would have a game of Charlemagne. If you have never played this card game, you are certainly missing something. It is the most popular game in the lumbering country and as old as the hills.

When the ice left the lakes I could go fishing again. I went on two camping trips into the Churchill area. Once we camped on Snare Brook while Dave attended to some lumber camps in that vicinity. On these trips I caught plenty of trout for our evening meals. Fishing was at its best.

In the early spring I love to hear the cheerful song of the frogs. And the soft quacking of young ducklings trailing their mother out on the lake. I have enjoyed the calls of the loons most of all, on a moonlit night, and by imitating their calls to my surprise after a while there would be several answering me. In the summer, there is the song of the crickets and the silent fireflies which cast a spark here and there in the darkness. Often a flying squirrel surprises you, flying in a fast circle above your head. Should your camp be near a river you will hear nothing else than the thunder of rapids, as the water flows over ledges and rocks.

The queerest noise back in the forest on a windy night are trees grown closely together; their branches rub against each other making a loud squeak like rusty hinges on a heavy door. The scream of a bobcat is very seldom heard. However, mingled with so many other noises that I don't know about, is the bark of a young fox and the cry of a deer or a cub bear which to me resemble the cry of a small child. But the sound I find the saddest is the hoot of an owl in the darkness as if a warning, and resembles the sounds of a man in distress back in a faraway swamp. When all is quiet, you hear the deer about your camp as they are curious animals; you may even hear them very close to you. But what I love best of all when I am alone in our camp is the thumping of rabbits' feet at my camp door. All this makes you wonder why the nights are not all alike, for some of the darkest nights I have known were dead silent.

In fall of 1933 our second child was born. Once again Dave had to be away and I went to have the baby at my mother-in-law's at Allagash. This time it was a boy. We named him Robert and later came to call him Bobby. He was a healthy baby, and two weeks after his birth I started for home camp. That month away from our home at Umsaskis was the longest month in my life. I was terribly lonesome for my husband and all the beauty that fall brings to the woodland near our cabin.

Chapter 6

My First Buck

It was getting near hunting season and people had started flowing in from all over, many from out of state. Camps were being prepared along the Lacroix road to take care of the hunters. The boardinghouse at Churchill Lake had all it could take care of, and Cook Poulin was all preoccupied with new recipes which would delight his hunters. Mrs. Massy had repaired the old Blanchette camp and was cooking for a dozen hunters. Ray and Dot Burnham at Clayton Lake were putting up their same old parties of years gone by. It was nice to meet the same people year after year and to see their smiling faces red with health and cold after a day's hunting. Every hunter looked his happiest when the deer hunting season opened. And I will match a hunter's appetite against a lumberman's any day of the year.

We had gone to Lac Frontiere to get a girl who would take care of the children and keep house for us. My husband was working most of the time now, and I, provided I could get our children taken care of, could accompany him wherever he went. For me, night patrol was very exciting. It is serious business watching for jackers, and some nights Dave had to travel many miles on foot, by water, and by car. I loved water patrols and car work by night, but I left the walking to Dave. Looking for loaded guns in cars is another of the warden's duties. It is surprising how many people seem to be unaware of the danger of loaded guns in cars and canoes.

At this season I was also able to hunt any time I felt like it. I loved partridges and did a lot of bird hunting. On many occasions when I went along with Dave these hunting forays took me away from the main road and provided an opportunity to see more of the wilderness than I would have otherwise.

One day on our way home from Clayton Lake we went back in the woods to look over a small brook that Dave had not visited since the early part of the summer and wanted to check. To his surprise the place had changed overnight, it seemed. Instead of a brook there was a good-size pond, and the cutting indicated that several beavers were at work gathering their winter food. A medium-size house was built on the south side of the pond, and by the size there could be perhaps six beavers. As we stood there looking over the place, a beaver swam ashore not too far from us, but the instant he got wind of us, he plunged, making a loud splash with his tail in a warning to the others that something was about.

Early one autumn morning the radio reports reminded me that there were only a very few days left until the close of the deer season. I decided then and there that not only was it high time I got my deer, but that I had best be getting on in earnest with my hunting. There had been some snow, and the threat of more—of much more—had driven most of the hunters out of the area back to their homes in Maine and other states. The chance of being snowbound is not one a hunter takes lightly.

After putting on all the warm clothes I possessed, I shut the radio off and hurried out, delighted with the day and the prospects it held. It was a clear, crisp morning and the light snowstorm of the day before, which had covered the dead leaves and dead branches on the ground, would help to choke the noises I would make while traveling through the woods.

Although I had been brought up in a family of ardent and successful hunters, I had never been much interested in traveling alone in the woods, and this time I would be all on my own. How and where I would shoot my buck I did not know. So here

I was, following an old tote road, moving cautiously along, and looking from one side to the other ahead of me. I finally reached the upper part of the ridge, where I thought I might regain my breath and sit and keep watch. I proceeded to move slowly from one tree to another until I found a proper place.

As I sat resting, the desire to see a deer right away became overwhelming, so I decided to keep on traveling. I moved cautiously again, this time keeping well bent over in an awkward and uncomfortable position. I would take a step, then transfer my weight to the other foot, and very slowly continue in that fashion until I was well over the ridge and soon to the edge of a growth of thick fir and old hardwood trees.

My husband had told me that during the day I would find the deer in the lowland area. I could see many tracks and felt certain I would see a deer. Then I decided I would pick a fresh track and follow it. My back was nearly broken from walking in such a cramped position, my .32 Winchester was getting heavier and heavier, and I was just beginning to feel sorry for myself and to wish my husband had come along with me, when suddenly I heard a thrashing in the thick growth of fir to one side. I turned quickly and got a glimpse of a big buck deer. He was unaware of me. Apparently I was doing all right despite my sore muscles and awkward bent-over manner of walking. I began to follow him, for I was certain he would stop after a time. I couldn't possibly get lost. With the snow on the ground I could retrack to the road I had just left. I went about two hundred yards more and stopped to listen.

Again I covered a similar distance and listened. No sound from the deer. Deer are funny animals. They are very acute. My husband had explained to me how deer will travel in a circle and lie back along their own trails and watch their enemy. I inched my way farther into the thickets and peered through the thick fir. I kept on inching forward, following the fresh deer tracks, and watching and listening for the least little noise. Now I noticed that the tracks were closer together. This meant the deer had stopped running. Bending to feel the deer's dropping I found it was warm. I knew then that the deer was not far ahead of me. I kept moving along automatically, fully expecting to come face to face with the deer at any moment.

Finally I reached a spot where the deer had lain for a few minutes. He was a big brute, I could tell by the imprint on the soft snow. I must, I thought, keep a sharp watch or I will be returning to camp with nothing but a story to tell. That I did not want to do—above everything. I seemed to be alone in the world, and the excitement I felt mounting within me developed into a steady beating at my temples. My tongue and mouth felt dry.

I continued to track the deer now, following an old trail. The going was easier here, but I was in more open country and could be seen more easily. But this did not last long. I soon reached the thickets again, this time through an old cutting going over dead logs which had fallen crisscross over one another. I collapsed in a heap between two dead logs, accidentally breaking some dry branches as I fell to the snow-covered ground. As I fell I heard a whistle, a loud whistle. It was my buck deer. From now on it was a dead buck or a shameful defeat for me.

At this moment I heard more thrashing and the breaking of frozen branches. I knew then that the deer had found another place to lie down and would now be on the watch for me. The sound was reassuring. Dropping on my hands and knees, and keeping my rifle from hitting the dead logs and low bushes, I finally reached another old deer trail. The fresh tracks still ahead of me were even closer together, and the going now was much easier. At last I reached the shelter of a large maple tree, which had fallen, leaving its roots standing about ten feet high. I stopped to rest. My watch said ten o'clock. The sun was warm at this time of day, but cold chills took hold of me nevertheless and my hands and feet were like ice. My knuckles were white from the death grip I had on my rifle.

Half an hour passed and my hopes were still high. I had the wild idea that the deer had known all along I was behind him. The thought that he had just been waiting and watching for my head to appear at that spot caused my hair to stand on end. An hour passed and not a sound came from the thickets. I was getting colder and colder. I got to my feet and slowly left my hideout. When I was once again on the trail the going was easy but quite open. Bending very low, I kept walking and looking all around me. I continued toward the swamp, and there I spotted more deer tracks. My plan of attack by then was casual. I had a hazy idea that perhaps I would soon come to the deer lick my husband and I had visited several times and maybe find my buck there. But instead the tracks circled around it and seemed to avoid this particular area.

The path I was following was getting very narrow. I had to bend very low in order to get by under the heavy, low branches. After a hundred yards or more of this kind of traveling I came upon a large spring. I could tell by the tracks that the deer had gone through it. I would have to beat my way around it, which would not be easy. The ground, which was soft and black and very muddy, wasn't frozen and my feet went deep into it. The mud slopped up over the tops of my boots and I could feel the water soaking through my stockings. I finally got a good hold on some roots and worked my way out, my hands dripping and my boots covered with a thick layer of mud. My rifle had become splattered, and I had a dreadful fear that it wouldn't fire now that I needed it so badly. Once I was on solid ground again I found the shelter of a large spruce and began cleaning my rifle.

The sights were filled with mud, but to my great relief I found that the barrel was clean and the shells dry.

After several minutes I got moving again. I wanted to make one more try before returning to the camp, but I had the awful feeling that my expedition was a failure. At this moment I saw one new track on the same path I was following. Then suddenly I came upon a large clearing where obviously there had once been a lumber camp. I stopped at the edge of the woods to study my surroundings, and as I stood there this whole stupid chase suddenly seemed like a crazy idea.

A second later I heard a soft little noise. Then, in a moment, it was repeated. It was followed by the rattling of horns, and there on the opposite side of the clearing I spotted two buck deer hooking their horns together. Was I to witness a battle between these two animals? My hopes instantly shot high as I realized I still had a chance—that the deer's suspicions must be temporarily allayed. Then a violent trembling took hold of me and it was all I could do to keep from crying. With all the willpower I had I pulled myself together. My heart was beating like a trip hammer from all the excitement and it was hard to think calmly.

The deer now appeared in the clearing, their horns clashing together in furious battle. They would fall and get up, fighting harder and harder to down one another. I didn't want to shoot just yet. I felt I was a little too far away. If only I could make my way nearer without being noticed. Slowly I inched myself along the edge of the clearing, and all at once, to my great surprise, I found myself face to face with a large doe. For a long time we stared at each other. She was standing absolutely still, and it looked as if every nerve in her body was focused right on me. Then suddenly her head turned, her eyes seemed to snap, and with a shake of her white flag she sounded the piercing whistle warning that an enemy was about. With that she disappeared among the thickets of fir and spruce.

For a brief instant time ceased to exist. It is hard to describe exactly what happened during the next minute or so. Everything must have taken place very quickly, but it seems that I was going almost as fast as the deer. Fifty yards away one of the bucks stopped, as if to keep guard and to reassure the others that all was well. I pushed the safety off and brought my rifle to my shoulder. The silence was rent by the explosion, but to my surprise the dazed deer continued to look all around. This gave me time to aim carefully for a second shot. This time he moved slowly to one side for a moment and then fell to the ground and lay still. He was done for, all right. I had not dreamed it would be possible for me to kill a deer all by myself, but here it was.

I looked about me and gradually a sense of reality returned to me. This was not the end. I had to bleed him if I wanted to save the meat. Taking my knife out of its sheath I began the operation, the blood oozing over my hand as I cut deep into his throat. Then I thought I had better remove the innards. I had never done that before, just as I had never cut a deer's throat. It was a new experience and one which I did not enjoy. I tried to turn the deer over so the blood would run out freely, but he was such a big brute that I could not do much. Afterward I used some snow to wash my hands as clean as I could. I dried them on my handkerchief.

By now my watch showed three o'clock. This was the time I was to have met my husband at the main road, and here I was—miles from the main road which itself was miles from our camp. It would be dark in a short time. If I didn't hurry I was in for it. I did not know how far back in the woods I had ventured. Following the deer had taken up all my attention. Fortunately

I still could see my tracks plainly as the sun began to set behind the ridge at my right. I started for home.

Keeping my eyes glued to my tracks and walking as fast as I could, I arrived at the spring I had had such a time crossing. Using both hands, and with a good foothold, I managed to scramble across without getting wet or soaked with the black mud. As I landed on the other side I heard someone calling. I knew it was my husband. As soon as he spotted me among the thick growth of fir branches he asked me if anything was wrong.

"Yes," I answered, "something is wrong, all right. I have shot a deer back half a mile. It will take a team of horses to haul it out of the swamp."

I could scarcely believe myself when I repeated for a second time that I really had shot my buck, bled him, and taken care of everything. I really felt proud of myself. I told my husband how it all had happened. Then we decided that we would return the next morning to get the carcass and haul it home. This was a lot of experience to cram into one day, and shortly after supper I retired for the night, too exhausted to do anything but drift off to sleep smiling contentedly over my day's adventure and looking forward to the next day.

Chapter 7

Keeping House

The hunting season over, I got busy preparing the meat for canning, and for mincemeat, which to my mind is best made with venison. Up to that time I had never made any mincemeat, so I began looking for a recipe. Most recipes I found required walnuts, wine, oranges, lemons, and whatnot. I closed the book, for only women in the city could make mincemeat like that. Then I thought of Maman Pacquet. We had eaten many of her tasty mince pies; they were delicious. So I called her and asked her if she would tell me how to make mincemeat, for I was ready to make it and did not know how. This is the recipe she gave me, the one I have used ever since.

3 bowls of chopped meat, cooked
1/2 bowl of vinegar
1 bowl of suet
2 bowls of raisins
2 tablespoons of nutmeg
5 bowls of apples
1 bowl of molasses
2 bowls of white sugar
2 tablespoons of cinnamon
2 tablespoons of cloves

Cook very slowly. Then put in jars while warm for preserving.

I have passed this recipe along to many and it has always been a great success.

The tender ribs of the deer can be canned, to be cooked as they are needed. You remove the rib bones and cut the meat into strips about three inches wide. Then for each strip add one teaspoonful of salt and a thin slice of salt pork rolled tight. Finally, put the strips in pint jars and steam them for three hours. Venison preserved in this way is excellent, and best of all, there is no waste.

I have often heard Levi Dow, my husband's supervisor, praise my venison meat, saying in his loud voice, "She can cook deer meat better than anyone I know. It just melts in your mouth."

During my second winter in the timberland I took to rug-making. At first, braiding a rug seemed quite a task, but once I learned the knack of doing it, it became very easy. The first three rugs I made we used at once. One went inside the front door, the next near our bed, the third in front of our sink. These added a cheery touch to our cabin. The one beside our bed felt so nice under our feet in the morning.

The winter was going by very fast. It seemed as if we had just gone through the hunting season and now it was almost Christmas and I had to look for a Christmas tree. Arlene was old enough now to be very much aware of the tree and her dolls, and even little Bobby would be excited by a sparkling tree in the house.

So one afternoon I went in search of a small full fir. They all looked very beautiful out there in the woods. I hated to cut one down, but just the same I did. It wouldn't be Christmas without a tree. While I decorated the small tree Dave made ice cream. He makes wonderful ice cream by combining a can of Eagle Brand milk, a can of Carnation milk, three well-beaten eggs, a cup of white sugar, a teaspoon of vanilla, and one can of fruit from which the syrup has been drained. This mixture is put into a freezer and stirred until it hardens.

On Christmas Eve, Father Du Lac came to Churchill to celebrate Midnight Mass at the boardinghouse. I wanted to go, so I asked Tom if he would look after the children. The services were very touching and Father Du Lac's sermon was wonderful. Quite a few lumbermen attended. I felt sorry for them—men who for some reason had not gone home for Christmas. No doubt there were loved ones who wished them home. After Father Du Lac's blessing we returned to our cabin.

The night was very cold and in the moonlight we could see every curve in the road ahead of us. The trees partly covered with snow cast their shadows here and there in the quietness of this large forest. We thought contentedly of the warm home waiting for us and our two beautiful babies.

I would not say that wintertime in the woods goes slowly. On the contrary, in no time you find that spring has already come. When my husband was home it was nice to be able to sit and talk, for our conversation never palled. There were hundreds of little things, interesting things, for us to talk about. For ourselves, at least, we proved that two people can live together very happily in the woods.

During the winter we sent away to Sears, Roebuck & Company for a fly-casting rod. The day we received it in the mail it was snowing quite hard. I hurried on my way back to have a look at this fly rod we had planned on buying for so long. I was alone at the camp that afternoon so I put the rod together and went out on the porch to try it out. I don't suppose I looked very sensible out there. But most people who live in the woods seem to enjoy doing things like that. I could hardly wait for spring. When Dave returned in the later part of the afternoon he saw that the rod had been put together. He looked at me, then at the rod, without saying a word.

"I wish you'd try it," I said.

The expression on his face changed to a broad smile, and he replied that he would rather wait for spring when fishing opened. But he put it together again and decided that it was a well-balanced rod and worth more than he had paid for it.

Dave suggested I take up fly tying. It would help to pass the time away and we would have plenty of flies to use for our summer fishing. We could also experiment with different flies. The next thing he did was to get me a fly-tying kit. When it came he made me a split-log shelf which I could use for fly tying and to fasten the vise on. Nothing is new about the idea.

So I set about learning to tie flies. It took a little while until I got the knack of holding the small feathers in place, but I managed to make several of them that day. Little did I think then that in my twenty years of living in the woods I would, as time went on, tie thousands of flies and turn a fascinating hobby into a productive little source of income. You sit at your worktable and renew memories of years gone by, of fishing expeditions of long ago, of the big ones you caught and the bigger ones that got away. I find it very relaxing.

When fishermen come up here the first thing they ask me is, "What's the best fly?" I can always name a few, and from my husband's great experience I have learned to identify and to make the best ones, the ones used most successfully. There are on the market, by the way, a great many patterns that are never used up here. In this region the parmachene belle is one of the most popular. It is made with a silver tag, a red and white tail, a yellow-floss body, a white hackle, and red and white wings. Flies with a little red, yellow, gray, and green are always in demand. The fish seem to like them. Dave uses a buck-tail all through the fishing season. This kind is made with deer hair. Generally it has a red body, though sometimes it is varied with green or yellow.

I recall a fishing trip I made one time on the St. John River. We chose a campsite along the way near a brook. Every now and then at sundown you could see some large trout jumping. I began to fish. For an hour I had no luck. I had tried every fly in the book. When I gave up Dave took over, but his luck was no better. While I was rearranging the flies in my book I noticed a number of little butterflies hovering above the wet ground on the shore. I picked one of them up. It was all black except for a little white edge around the wings. Dave came by as I was examining this little fellow and he stopped, picked one up himself, baited his hook with it, and cast his line into the brook. It had no more than touched the water when he hooked a ten-inch trout. Turning toward me he said, "Pass me another one of those." I soon found myself chasing butterflies along the shore. It was worth the running, as each one brought a trout. We had not only enough for supper but plenty for our breakfast as well.

In February, I began to wish I had a sled on which to take the children out. They were growing rapidly. Arlene was walking. Bobby was a beautiful baby with big blue eyes and curly hair. So far we had been fortunate; neither one of them had ever been sick.

The trail to the main road where we went after our mail every day was very good. And the trail across the lake was always good. On a lake where the wind packs the snow as hard as a summer road I knew I would enjoy it, and it would be fun to go around the lake on a sunny day. If I only had a sled. Dave told me that on our next trip to Lac Frontiere we would look for a sled. A few days went by. Then my brother sent word that his dogsled was for sale. It was a wonderful sled; it was made of dry hardwood and weighed only seventeen pounds. This sled was about five feet long and about eighteen inches wide. The runners were well turned up and extended behind the back of the sled a good fifteen inches where part of it was flattened so I could stand on the runners. On each side of the back there were two handles; the bottom of the sled and the backrest were laced with snowshoe lacing. Dave made side boards for it about four inches high so the children could be tucked in it for warmth. It was, in one word, a regular Eskimo sled as I had seen many times in magazines.

I had a fur rug that I used in the bottom of this sled to make it more comfy. Every now and then I took the children out when the weather permitted. We went on the trail which took us to the main road, and often we would get there in time to pick up our mail which was left in a small box by the side of the road. Some days when the wind wasn't blowing we went on the lake. The trails were made by going over them first on snowshoes several times. The snow packed easily and became a hard-crusted trail. Thereafter, unless more snow falls, snowshoes are not needed. If the wind was blowing we used the trails through the woods. Arlene liked the woods trails the best. Every time we got ready she kept asking to go in that direction.

These woods trails took us up along the ridge back of our camp, then made a circle around through a thick growth of fir and spruce. Often we saw a pair of snowshoe rabbits or perhaps a few partridges picking at the bark of the trees. Toward spring our trails became soft and we could no longer go on them. Because of the wet thaw we soon missed our outdoor hour each day.

Although Tom was living at his camp near ours that winter, he frequently went back and forth between Umsaskis and Clayton Lake to check his traps. Almost every day he stopped at our cabin, sometimes to visit for several hours. For Dave this winter was very much like the previous ones. There were some new lumber camps in new locations, but basically he simply continued doing what he had done in the past. There were many men roaming the timber cuttings and Dave's job was to check them. Among the woodsmen this year were several from the Allagash Plantation. Most people called these fellows "Moose-towners." Walter Kasey was one of these. He had been born and brought up close to Dave and they had worked together for many years. On Sundays he often came to our cabin for dinner. We enjoyed his visits, for he is a good storyteller.

I still don't know which I prefer—summer with its fishing and camping and the other good things it has to offer, or winter when after a trip through the snow with the children and the dogsled our little cabin was the coziest place in the world. I do know that I loved the days when the blizzards came and if you looked out the window you could see nothing but drifting snow for miles on the wide lake. The snow would cover up all signs of the trail to the main road and the paths to the water hole and the woodshed. Outside there would be nothing but a blanket of white, white snow.

Sometimes I have seen these blizzards last three or four days at a time. Every once in a while you'd open the door a crack to look outside and a big gust of wind would whirl a powdery column of snow through the door and into your face. With the temperature twenty-five degrees below zero you slam the door in a hurry, slide the handwrought bolt into its groove as if you were barricading your home against intruders, and rush back to the stove to throw in some more wood. This is the time of year when it is particularly good to have a well-stacked bookshelf within reach.

One of the richest pleasures I know of is being housebound because of the wild winter weather outside. With your family about you, a good book on your lap, a roaring fire in the stove, and a good hot dinner in prospect—you are richer than a million-aire. There is no use in looking at the clock during a blizzard, for then time means nothing. In the wilderness, in an odd way, this sense of timelessness occurs at other times throughout the year as well. Many times, watching my children play on the floor by the fire, I have wished the blizzard would last days longer.

The snow does queer things to the forest. After the storm is over and the sun begins to shine, everything you gaze upon glitters like small diamonds. The huge pine tree which before the snow had stood tall and black against the winter sky, and the shorter spruce trees and thick-boughed firs, are completely covered with snow. Sometimes the tiptops of the trees shake off their snowcaps so that they look like big, round-shouldered snowmen with little black hats on their heads. You find yourself picking out curious resemblances between the snow shapes and houses or castles or mountain peaks. Places which once looked as if they might have been good hideouts for small animals or birds are completely covered. The hardwood trees, bare of their beautiful green and yellow and red autumn dress, stand erect and snow-streaked. Under the heft of new snow some of them are bending close to the breaking point.

The Humane Society sent my husband three traps for him to use as an experiment. They were for small animals and were different from other traps; they would capture the animals instead of killing them. One day he set the three of them along the road going to Priestly Lake; bobcats were very thick in that area. Each day I visited the traps, but the storms which came so fast and furiously made it almost impossible to keep them free of ice and snow, and the winter went by without the capture of a single animal.

We once, however, had a run-in with a bobcat. One winter day as Dave was splitting a block of wood beside the camp door, I came out for a bit of conversation and looking out over the lake, noticed a dark moving object in the distance. It was following a track made several days before by one of Blanchette's men. I motioned to Dave to look. He said he thought it was a dog, but as it came closer he said, "No, it's a bobcat. Get me the rifle, quick."

I rushed into the camp and returned with the rifle and three cartridges. By that time the bobcat had gone down the hill to the shore of the lake. Dave grabbed the rifle and dashed off through the woods toward the lake shore with our dog Kate bounding along beside him. I had often heard Dave say that in all his life he had never shot a bobcat, so I knew how anxious he must be to get this one. A few moments later I heard a shot, then another, then a third. I ran toward the lake to a point where I could see Dave. He was waving his arms, making signs for me to come. I still could see the cat ahead of him.

I gathered the remaining five cartridges which had been left from our most recent hunting trip, got the kiddies settled in the window, and told them to watch Mommy and Daddy and to be very quiet until we returned. I followed the trail a way, then cut across toward Dave and the bobcat. The cat still sat a good fifty feet away, eyeing Dave and the dog as they waited for me. All out of breath from running, I handed Dave the five .32 specials. He loaded, pumped five shots at the cat—and never hit him. I was really cross for once.

"What are you going to do now?" I said.

Dave looked exasperated and replied that there must be something wrong with the rifle.

I reminded him that he had shot his deer last fall with it.

Just as I was saying this, Kate jumped on the cat, and the cat and dog went into a wild, thrashing tussle. Sometimes the cat was on top, sometimes it was Kate. They were covered with slush and blood and we felt sure we were going to lose Kate. But then suddenly the cat did not want to fight anymore. I looked at Dave and saw at once that something was brewing in his mind.

The cat had gone back a way to lie down and lick its wounds. All of a sudden Dave lunged at the animal and whacked it over the head with the butt of his rifle. He fetched it such a blow that the cat practically disappeared under the snow. All I could see of it was a little patch of fur. With the rifle in one hand Dave stooped down, picked up the cat by a hind leg, and began walking home.

It took only a few minutes for the cat to begin to come to, and the next thing we knew he was clawing at Dave's leg. This called for some quick thinking and quick action on Dave's part. He tried to keep the cat from clawing his leg by staving it off with the butt of his rifle, but this didn't work. Finally he whirled the cat around a few times by the hind leg and banged its head with the butt of his rifle. Thereafter he dragged the cat, head down, through the slush until we got home. The bobcat weighed about thirty pounds and sopping wet, it weighed a lot more. By the time we got home, Dave's arm was almost as dead as the cat.

We skinned the cat, dried the pelt, and then tanned it. We rubbed in quantities of coarse salt to help remove the fat and then, using a solution of alum powder, washed the pelt thoroughly. This washing disposed of the last traces of fat and preserved the hide. The fur was thick and soft and very dark gray in color. For a while the pelt hung on the wall over our couch, but then we took it down and stored it away. I forget now what has become of it.

February makes its appearance one bright sunny morning, but before we even have a chance to size up the month on the calendar it is time to tear off the page and take a look at March. I think that one of the things which makes winter seem to go so quickly is the crazy changes of weather you experience: beautiful days followed by nasty ones, sun followed by snow, calm followed by raging winds.

Unexpectedly, during a trip to Depot Lake, Dave and another game warden named Wilson from Nine Mile caught two young deer killers red-handed. The young men, with a big sledload of venison hauled by four good, rugged dogs, were heading for the Canadian border. The meeting with Dave and Wilson threw these culprits into such a state of fright that they just stood there trembling, unable to whisper a word. Dave and Wilson placed them under arrest and started to lead them to the nearest court, seventy miles distant at St. Francis, way up to the northeast. They covered this distance on snowshoes, following the Big Black, the St. John, and the Allagash rivers, thence to St. Francis.

They turned the deer slayers over to the judge at St. Francis and made the return trip again on snowshoes. All in all, the round trip of over a hundred and fifty miles was an exhausting expedition for these two wardens. The weather that March, with rains and thaws and blustery winds, was miserable. I think that anyone who accomplishes a snowshoe trip of that length under such conditions deserves a medal. But game wardens get no medals.

My own most grueling winter experience happened on the water. It was early winter of another year and Dave had to check on a lumber camp which had recently begun operations in the St. John River-PocWoc Stream area, and we set out in cold, fair weather after hearing over the radio that the forecast for the next few days was continued fair and cold. Nevertheless, we wore our rough-weather clothing—heavy breeches, rubber boots, parkas, and mittens. The water was high enough for good outboarding and I settled in the bow of the canoe, prepared for a chilly but interesting ride. The bow rode high enough so that I didn't get much spray, but Dave, in the stern, got a thorough sopping. When we arrived at the Castongay settlement on the St. John River at dusk, we found that several men had arrived there before us that day. Consequently we spent the night in our sleeping bags on the floor.

The next morning the caretaker's dog awakened me by licking my face, and Dave and I got up to discover that while the weather appeared to be warmer than the day before, a fine mist was falling. We ate breakfast, packed, and once again set out for the little game warden's camp on the Big Black. It was deserted when we got there several hours later, and Dave spent the rest of the day getting the camp into shape for the winter—chopping and stacking wood, patching a portion of the roof, tightening window frames, and so on.

I cooked supper and we then turned in for the night. A few hours later I was awakened by a howling wind that threatened to dislodge the tin stovepipe, which projected through the roof, from the little potbellied stove. I got up to take a peek out the window and saw that snow was being blown about at a terrific rate. And since there was nothing better I could do about it, I crawled back into my sleeping bag and slept soundly through the rest of the night.

The next morning was bleak and cold and the ground was covered by a heavy blanket of snow. While I prepared a hefty breakfast of bacon and eggs and coffee, Dave went outside and brushed our canoe free of snow. After eating we packed our duffel, loaded the canoe, locked up the camp, and set out on the St. John River, which by now was more slush than water. About a half-hour after we left the shore in front of the camp our outboard conked out. The gray slush in the river had been too much for it and the gas line had frozen up tight. Dave yanked at the lanyard a few times, but when it became apparent that we had a dead motor, he paddled over to the shore and beached the canoe in six inches of snow.

Then he got out his ax, chopped some branches, and after spilling a bit of gas on them got a roaring fire going. We huddled up close to it while he took the gas line apart and thawed it out. After drying it as thoroughly as possible he reassembled the motor. Then we buried the fire in the snow and set out once again. But the cards were stacked against us that day. We had gone only a little way farther when the motor began to heat up and then to sputter. Finally it stopped dead once again.

Since paddling in all that slush was next to impossible, Dave got out the canoe pole and tried to push us forward with that. It was terribly difficult going, for although the snow had stopped, the wind was still blowing a gale and the slush was so thick by now that the canoe seemed to weigh a ton. Furthermore, it was cold and windy as only the north woods can get. Several hours of this is about as much as a human being can take.

Finally we came in sight of Morel Shed. Here in this wide area of dead water there was only a tiny channel still unfrozen. We had a fierce time working our way through this, for the hardened ice seemed somehow to crowd against us. At one point the low gunwale of our canoe got caught under a ledge of it, and the next thing we knew we had shipped a mess of slushy water. We would have been lost had we shipped much more, for we were far from shore in that wide area and had we had occasion to call out for help, no one could possibly have heard us, so loudly was the wind blowing.

Drenched now and frightfully uncomfortable in the icy wet bottom of the canoe, we continued on toward the camp inhabited by the Mullins, a woods couple we knew, seven miles or so down the river. By now the gunwales of the canoe were hidden under three inches of ice, Dave's parka was frozen stiff as a board, and I was so cold I had all I could do to keep my teeth from clacking. Nevertheless we pushed on—Dave pushed us on—and after what seemed like an eternity, we sighted Mullins' camp.

After another eternity we came abreast of it, but it was not possible to push or paddle ourselves in to the shore. Except for the tiny free area in the middle where our canoe lay, the river was solidly frozen. Very warily—and how he did it in his half-frozen condition, I don't know—Dave worked his way over the gunwale of the canoe onto the ice, and then testing the solidness of the ice in front of him by rapping it with his ax, he made his way in to the shore. Having determined that the ice was firm enough to walk on, he came back to the canoe and helped me out. Between us we managed to drag the canoe to the shore, where we left it. Dave, I remember, said, "I don't care if it stays there until July."

Then we continued up the bank to the Mullins' camp which, with smoke pouring out of its chimney, looked like heaven on earth to us.

Mrs. Mullin greeted us with, "Well, for God's sake! You two *would* be out on a day like this."

We must have been a sight. I know for sure that Dave was. His eyebrows were white with frost as was the fur around the hood of his parka. Even his face, except for two small melted areas around his mouth and nostrils, was covered with ice and snow. And he actually had icicles hanging on his chin where the dampness of his breath had been caught for a moment and frozen. They looked like the grayish beard of an old man.

The Mullins' cabin was as warm and pleasant as a good dream, and Mrs. Mullin—"Mealy"—went to work on us immediately. Our fingers were too stiff to be of any use, so she unbuttoned our outer clothing, helped us out of it, and then drew two chairs up close to the hot fire. There we sat shivering for a while, working our fingers and toes to get the circulation active again. Mealy brought us hot broth and warm bread which we ate there before the fire, and after we had thawed out enough to be able to move about, she insisted that we turn in to get ourselves thoroughly warm and to avoid catching bad colds.

By this time it was early evening and we didn't need much urging. We did as we were told, and the next thing we knew the sun was shining and a new day—a Sunday—had dawned. We felt no bad aftereffects of the awful experience of the day before. In fact, we both felt fine.

Mealy made one of her wonderful Mulligan stews, and we piled into it so ravenously that she must have been astonished. However, her stew is so good that I think even a man who wasn't hungry would eat it with gusto. We were sorry that her husband wasn't there to enjoy it with us. He was off working at a lumber camp deep in the woods.

The following day, the last day of the hunting season, I went hunting while Dave cached our canoe, tent, sleeping bags, and lunch box. I might as well have stayed at camp. I shot nothing. Threatening weather kept us at the Mullins' camp for two more days.

While I am writing about the Mullins' camp, I must mention something Dave told me about after one of his stays there another time when he'd been out making inspections.

One day he asked Mealy if she had gotten the day's news over her radio.

"You know, the radio is no good at all these days," she replied.

Dave took that to mean either that the radio was out of order or that atmospheric conditions made reception poor. However, a while later Mealy phoned her sister, who lived three miles away. Among other things, they talked about radio programs, and when Mealy hung up she rushed to the radio and turned it on.

"Annie says they're playing all kinds of fiddle pieces," she said.

Sure enough, a moment later the room was full of music out of a radio that worked perfectly. Apparently, in Mealy's opinion, a radio was no good unless you could get fiddle music out of it.

On Thursday, Dave and I set out to walk the sixteen or so miles which separated us from our home. I carried my rifle; Dave carried on his back a pack containing all the things we would need for the trip. There wasn't much of a road to follow—a narrow little path beaten down in the snow by the feet of the few trappers and woodsmen who had passed along this route. Even so, Dave figured out a shortcut we could take to a little village where we could hire a car to carry us to the ferry station across the river from our community. The sight of the bateau in the slushy river gave me a sickening feeling—but we made the trip across without incident, and just a little while later had our arms around our happy children in our own house. It was good to be home.

In March during the breakup spell we decided to wash the logs inside our camp, using steel wool and good soapy water. In two days this was done and the logs became a bright and shiny gold color. We also decided—come summer—to make a new addition to the main camp, an extra room which could be used either as a bedroom or kitchen. I was pretty happy about this plan, as it was quite a problem to keep things in shape in so small a place. I didn't like, for instance, having to put clothes in boxes under our bed. This necessity involved me in a lot of guesswork, for every time I needed some clothes I had to get down on my knees and begin to haul out boxes. The first one I withdrew was certain not to be the one I was looking for. And out would come another, and another, until the six boxes and the two suitcases we possessed were out from under the bed. It seemed that whatever I needed was always in the farthest corner of the bottom of the last box. So one day I made up my mind that something must be done and a new system adopted.

It was like this. The two suitcases contained our best clothes. On the cover of each box I listed the contents, using for ink some bright-red nail polish someone had given me. I put each child's clothing in a separate box. Then I stored the boxes under our bed again. Contents were clearly marked. That problem was solved.

I also had difficulty keeping track of the family's stockings. Living in very small quarters as we do and having, for the most part, to make shift with fairly slim pickings—there are no department stores in the wilderness—one has to puzzle out many things for better housekeeping. One's ingenuity and resourcefulness are frequently strained to meet the everyday problems of keeping order.

One day when we went to Blanchette's lumber camp I asked the clerk at the office if he had a box just so large, a wooden box. Glad to be of any assistance to the game warden's wife, he rushed into the shed and returned a moment later with an empty butter box. These boxes are waxed inside and made of four-ply veneer. It was just the right size. I thanked him very much and hurried back home. The next day while I was all alone I made a skirt to go around it with some bright cretonne I had. I added two small hinges to keep the cover on permanently. Then I padded the top and covered it with more cretonne. In went the stockings and the stocking problem was finally solved. The box serves too as a handy little footrest near our rocking chair.

Chapter 8

Bear Stories

I had developed a fear of bears, probably from having listened to too many woodsmen's stories about them. One, for example, was about the time Mrs. Gus Bernier at Nine Mile over on the St. John River baked a batch of raisin bread and set it to cool on a table in front of a window. She went to the back of her cabin to fetch a cloth to put over her loaves, and when she returned there was a huge bear in the window helping himself to a fresh loaf. She let out what must have been a record-breaking scream. The bear fled into the woods. This and many similar stories had finally made a haunting impression on me.

My husband remarked many times that there was no danger, and I had never told him of my worries. I realized that in his work, the thought of leaving his family alone for days on end was hard enough without his having to concern himself with my terror of bears. Nevertheless, the fear has never left me.

In some ways, bears are funny animals. They rarely harm anyone, and more often than not if they see you they run so fast you hardly have a chance to look at them. They make their dens in the early part of the fall, choosing a big cedar or pine whose roots are off the ground, and use birch and cedar bark to pad their nest. They grind this as fine as silk, line their den with it, and then barricade the opening.

The birth of one to three cubs near the end of the hibernation period does not greatly disturb the long sleep of the she-bear. Her six-month fast has kept the young ones small. At birth they rarely weigh more than a pound and sometimes as little as two ounces. But when the family emerges in the spring sunlight, the cubs soon suckle themselves to chubbiness. Then there are lessons in tree climbing and hunting. Transgressions in behavior bring a sharp rap across the snout from mama bear. Despite the intimacy with their mother during childhood, the cubs are on their own at the next winter. Should their paths later cross, mother and children would pay little attention to each other.

I listened one day to a trapper telling my husband about an experience he had had with a bear. While looking over his trap line he had noticed some black hair in a small opening of a dry cedar near by. Upon examining it closely he had decided there was a bear hibernating in the hollow tree. With the handle of his ax he poked at it and discovered that the bear was alive. Without further ado he shot the bear. Then he cut the cedar down. As he split the dry tree open it became apparent that the bear was wedged in it. The animal had forced its way into the dry trunk in the early part of the fall, and then, oddly enough, had grown during the winter. Had the trapper not shot it, the bear would have had to gnaw its way out in the spring.

I will never forget the first tangle I had with a bear. We had built a little greenhouse about twenty feet from our cabin—made camp-fashion of small logs covered with hand-split shingles. "Greenhouse" is the backwoods name for a cold cellar. It was about ten feet square and banked all around with earth. This banking kept the place very cold and provided an excellent storage place for perishable food such as butter, lard, bacon, ham, and some canned foods.

One night when all was quiet I settled down with a book to read. All of a sudden I heard shingles being torn off the greenhouse. I sat up in bed, wondering at first if I'd heard what I thought I'd heard or if it was only my imagination. Anyway, my heart was pounding and my thoughts were all bear. I finally got up and went to the window. It was a moonlit night and I could see quite well outside except in the shadowy patch of trees surrounding the greenhouse. Once or twice I rapped on the window and still the noise continued. The third time, to my terror, I saw a huge bear jump off the top of the greenhouse and scramble down the path toward the lakeshore. My rifle, a .32 Winchester, stood loaded at the head of our bed. However, it never occurred to me to use it. All I was interested in was scaring off the bear—the farther and faster the better. I didn't want to have to get close enough to him to shoot.

I took a long time getting back to sleep that night. I started a fire, made some coffee, and turned on the radio. Every once in a while I would turn the radio off and listen with my ear pressed against the door or window frame. It was three in the morning when I decided to go back to bed. For a last time I took a look outside. The sky was lighter now and it would soon be daylight. To my amazement I saw five deer feeding around the cabin. A buck feeding near the edge of the road seemed to be keeping guard over the others. Then I noticed something very curious about one of the deer—a doe: she was walking on three legs. One shriveled front leg was hanging oddly. The base of the good front leg seemed to have worked its way over toward the middle of the chest to make balance easier. I stood at the window, watching the deer feed on the newly grown clover and pausing every once in a while to lift their heads. The deformed doe had no doubt been wounded by a hunter and had managed not only to get away but to forage and do pretty much what the other deer did despite her handicap. The sight of the deer reassured me and I went to bed, certain that my bear was a long way off by then.

When I awoke the next day, my first look at the greenhouse told me that I might very well find all our food gone. But instead, only the shingles were torn off the roof. I had scared him just in time, but I was certain he would be back. When, I did not know. When my husband returned this was my first and most important piece of news for him. He said the bear would be back soon, since he had smelled the food. When he asked me if I had been frightened I answered no. I was still determined never to tell him that now more than ever I was terrified of bears. Once more the bear stories had been renewed in my mind.

Our dog, Kate, a husky, all black with a white breast and two white paws, was a good dog, and I must confess that though I said nothing about it then, I found considerable relief in the thought that she might give me a warning each time a bear might come along. It was Kate, however, who gave away to my husband the carefully guarded secret of my fear of bears. Always when he asked me, I used to say, "No—I am not afraid of bears." Then one night when he came home late from a trip up to the Musquacook Lakes, he found me sound asleep in a chair, hanging on to Kate's collar. She had become for some reason very shy and would hide under the bed. In order to keep her out that night I had held her by her collar. Then Dave knew that I was afraid of bears.

The lumber camps had quite a time dealing with bears. The food supplies at the camps were neatly stored away and one man, usually an old woodsman, was hired to look after the camp and supplies. Often this caretaker wouldn't be able to frighten the bear away, for all the fine scents such as coffee, molasses, sugar, raisins, prunes, and dry apples were such a temptation to "Mr. Bear." So the caretaker would telephone Dave to ask his help. Toward evening my husband would go up. Just at twilight the bear would make his appearance.

I recall one time when Dave got such a call to go to Blanchette's camp, which was situated along the main road between Umsaskis and Churchill. Dave suggested that I take the kiddies and come along since it was such a nice evening. When we arrived just at dusk, he parked the car a few feet from the cook room and put up the car windows to keep out the mosquitoes, which were terrible. While I settled in the car for a good long wait, Dave went to the cook room to talk to the caretaker about the bear. Bobby was on my lap nearly asleep when little Arlene suddenly stood up on the seat behind the steering wheel and pointed her finger to the opposite side of the car, her eyes as big as saucers. To my horror I could see outlined against the edge of the woods the caretaker's visitor—a huge black bear walking in leisurely fashion toward the storehouse. I took Arlene by the arm and drew her to my side, putting my finger to my lips to shush her. We were both fascinated, wondering what the bear would do if he noticed the car. Repeating the sign of no noise to Arlene, I watched breathlessly as the bear approached the car. He lumbered up to it, stood up on his hind legs, and began sniffing.

I was terrified. He was now so near that at the least little noise he might have jumped and with his great paws broken the windows. It was barely dark and in the twilight we could see him plainly. His eyes were very small, considering the size of his head. His ears stood up, and while he sniffed he made a little grunting noise with his nose. It is impossible now for me to put down on paper the fear I felt at that moment. After he had satisfied himself in this harmless way that nothing was amiss, he got down on all fours and made his way to the storehouse.

I began to honk the horn frantically and Dave came out on the run. I was unable to speak when he opened the door of the car, and all I could do was make a sign toward the storehouse. But Arlene said in a whisper, "Bear, Daddy." Dave put a cartridge in his rifle and headed toward the rear of the storehouse. In a second we heard the noise of the rifle shot. We knew then that Mr. Bear was no more. Later when I had a chance to examine him as he lay stretched out behind the storehouse, I realized what a good sound basis there had been for my terror. He was a big brute. Dave said he weighed over three hundred pounds.

The caretaker was very happy. He would be able to sleep this night without disturbance. But all those bear stories renewed themselves in my mind still again. What's more, now I knew that they were all true. Next morning we returned to help dispose of the bear. At this time of year, unfortunately, the fur was of no value.

On another occasion, when Dave was away, I went out to our greenhouse to get some milk for breakfast. I found the place a shambles. What we had had on the shelves was strewn on the ground. Our butter had been tramped down. The pail of lard was half empty and the bone was all that remained of the big ham we had just bought. Only the canned milk and canned fruits remained untouched on the shelves.

I bolted back to the camp calling for Jeanne, a young friend who was then staying with me, to come quick. Together we returned to the greenhouse to investigate. We found huge bear tracks in the soft earth outside and followed these back toward the main road, past the front of the garage within a few feet of our camp. Jeanne and I finally stopped and looked at one another wide-eyed, thinking how close he must have been the night before. We decided that he had done his damage while we had had the radio on loud. That bear must have liked music and we really must have had the radio turned up high, for without hearing him do it he had torn off a large section of roof on one side of the greenhouse. Judging by the size of the hole he made, we guessed that he was enormous. In any case, he made plenty of room for himself to go in and out.

That evening I called Bert Duty's camp at Eagle Lake on the telephone to tell Dave about it. Bert told me they were just having dinner and telling each other bear stories, while a couple of fishermen listened, goggle-eyed.

I said, "I have a real bear story to tell Dave, if I may speak with him."

Then I told Dave my story and he told me to meet him at Churchill wharf after supper. He also said that one of the fishermen wanted to come along to see the bear. So we spent most of that evening listening to this fisherman, a New York reporter, who had many interesting things to tell about, more interesting—as far as we were concerned—than our bear incident. He'd stay up all night, he said, to see the bear. However, Dave told him that he did not think the bear would be back, for after a big feed bears don't usually show up for about a week. But he insisted, so we let him watch. When I got up the next morning for the baby's feeding, he was still at his post on the back porch. If by any chance the bear had returned to the greenhouse he would have turned back after seeing someone sitting there on the back porch. But the reporter enjoyed his night's watch. It was all a new experience for him in this big wilderness.

The next morning my husband said he would set a bear trap, using the remains of ham and what was left of the lard and butter. Dave set off and the fisherman and I followed. We went over the ridge and down into the thicket.

If you haven't seen a bear trap set, you have missed something very interesting. Setting a bear trap, by the way, is not as easy as one might think. To find the right spot is the first step. The steel bear trap itself weighs some forty pounds. Its huge jaws are about twelve inches long, with heavy springs on each side. The springs are so tight that it is very difficult for one man to set the trap alone. When set, the trap is fastened to a tree by a three-foot length of chain. The bait is placed a few inches inside the trap. The place one chooses does not matter a great deal if the bear has never been in the area: the smell of the bait will bring him in time. Once the trap is set, the jaws and spring are covered lightly with some moss and a fence of some kind is built on each side of the trap to protect people who might go by this same spot. Knowing a trap was set, I felt pretty safe when we returned to the camp. I was sure that in time we would outwit the bear.

Dave and the reporter went back to Churchill, and Jeanne, the children, and I were once again left alone. One night all was quiet, and we were just about ready to drop off to sleep, I heard a *thump-thump-thump* down the road. Jeanne and I didn't get up. We just lay there still as pictures on the wall. By and by the thumping suddenly ceased. I thought it might be a moose, for I did not know then that bears make such a racket when traveling through the woods. After investigating the next morning we found the imprint of a large bear's paws in the soft ground in front of our garage.

Again I called my husband at Bert's camp and told him of the heavy thumping on the road and of the huge bear tracks just by the garage. He said he would try to come down as soon as possible. We drove to Churchill Lake to get him later that evening.

Louis Pacquet dropped by the next morning just when Dave was ready to go look at the bear trap. So they went off together. As they neared the place they stopped to listen. They heard growls and thrashing about in the thicket and they knew then that Mr. Bear had fallen for the bait. There he was in the trap, a huge brute, three hundred pounds of him. After a few minutes of watching him try to pull away from the trap, Dave shot him. It was quite a task to haul this big fellow back to the cabin, but Dave and Louis finally made it. We took pictures and we kept Mr. Bear around for a few days for the sake of visitors who might want to get a look at him. He got smelly, however, and we had to bury him.

Chapter 9

The Spring of the Year

E ver since I can remember I cannot help looking toward the
sky and listening to the first springtime quacking of ducks
flying out over the lake. At our camp door the moose birds are
noisier than ever, while the squirrels in the maple trees, as I go
out to the main road for our mail, are chattering louder, going
from one tree to the other. Although the snow is still deep, the
air I feel on my face is different. And I know then from long
experience that it will soon be time to tap the sugar maples.

It took me back to when I was a child living at Seven
Islands. My father had what we all called a "sugary." This was a
very large cabin which he had built two miles from our house for
the purpose of sugar making. Close by it he had built a smaller
cabin to live in during the sugaring.

In those days he used pails made out of birch bark. He
called these *casseaux*. The birch bark was gathered in the first
part of August and stored away. Toward spring he would make
the pails. Each took a large piece of bark about thirty inches
long and about twenty-five inches wide. This was heated flat
on a warm stove to make it pliable. Then the ends were folded
square and held together with little wooden pegs. He used a wire
to make a handle so it could be hung on the maple tree. When
the tree was tapped he used little wooden pipes to guide the sap
into the *casseaux*.

He gathered sap from these *casseaux* and transferred it into
two barrels which would hold fifty gallons each. By means of a
dog team and a narrow sled the barrels were then transported
to the camp, where the sap was boiled down. To boil the sap

my father used a vat which was fifteen feet long, four feet wide, and fifteen inches deep. This was set on a specially constructed fireplace where a fire burned continuously. The sap was boiled down to a thin syrup, then the syrup was removed, transferred into a large iron pot, and cooked until it became either a thick syrup or sugar, whichever was preferred.

One gathers more sap when the nights are warm and the days are sunny. Very cold frosty nights stopped the sap from running. The best sugar and syrup are made in the first part of the sugar season; toward the end, when the snow has melted and the days are warm, the sap gathered then makes a very dark sugar which tastes as if it had been burned. Should you sell this the value of it is very low. Since my father's childhood days the making of the sugar was very simple to him, and by the gathering of the sap he could well tell just how much sugar he could make with each gallon of sap.

The trails through the maple trees are made on snowshoes first as the trees are being tapped. After snowshoes have pounded down the trails a few times the snow becomes packed and frozen and enables the dogs and the sleds to pass over them with much less danger of spilled loads.

In later years my father purchased an up-to-date vat and shiny galvanized pails. Instead of dogs and sled he used a team of horses. And then instead of tapping three hundred maples he tapped twenty-five hundred. He sold a great amount of syrup and sugar to the buyer every spring.

Outsiders think all there is to sugaring, from one year to the next, is tapping the trees and making the sugar. But there is more to it than just that. In early fall my father and one hired man would go to the sugary for two solid weeks' work among the maple trees. Some maples had to be cut down because they had too many broken limbs or because rot had set in. A lot of underbrush had to be cleared out to make the going better while the trees were being tapped. Some had to be cut down and saved for firewood. There were repairs to be made on the camp itself, and utensils to be cleaned and polished.

Soon after my father started gathering sap, the three of us— my mother, my father, and I—always had a sap-gathering party. We took the first syrup and dropped little pools of it on the snow. In no time it turned into hard candy, sticky to be sure, but very tasty. We also made from the first syrup a batch of sweet dumplings. To my mind these were the best sweets I ever ate. This is how my mother cooked them. She put one quart of syrup into a large saucepan. Then she mixed two cups of white flour, a pinch of salt, two teaspoons of baking powder, and two eggs, adding just enough water to make a thick batter. When the syrup was boiling she dropped in the batter spoonful by spoonful. And when the dumplings were done they were a golden brown and melted in your mouth.

Something I used to enjoy was making little cones out of birch bark. When my father was ready to pour the maple sugar into the molds, he filled my cones too. My cones were of various sizes, some just large enough to hold a bite. I have, for years, kept one as a token. I also greatly enjoyed wandering idly through the maple grove at this season, as I used to see a great many birds that stay around the region all winter.

I like to watch them, because at this time of the year they are nesting and are hungrier than ever; if we put out some food, they carried away as much as they could, hiding it in some hundred places which later is found by squirrels who get fat on it. The moose birds are so tame by then they will come eat from your hand.

Once every spring we had a large party. My mother and father would invite all the neighbors. Father would make a big batch of sugar. There would be games and singing, a wonderful lunch, and all the maple candy anyone wanted. Although these parties occurred many years ago, people still talk of them. Certainly I will never forget them. My mother and I loved to sit by the camp door in late afternoon and listen to the sap falling into the newly emptied pails. It sounded very gay tinkling through the maple grove. The air filled our lungs with the sweet scent of the sap as we watched the steam escaping in clouds from the boiling vat.

Now that the snow had gone and the lakes were free of ice again, it was nice to see the blue water. In late spring everyone went fishing. I liked to take the children and go to the mouth of Drake Brook to fish the trout there that rarely ran under a pound and had lovely dark pink flesh. Occasionally we would go plug fishing. This is less exciting, but fun even so. You use a heavy line with a sinker on the end and a large hook fastened close to the sinker. You bait the hook with a five-inch live chub. After your canoe is anchored you let down your line until you hit bottom. Then you sit quietly until you have a bite. This procedure is followed for the simple reason that large fish lie on the bottom—it is cooler there. You must remain absolutely quiet, and you may have to wait a full hour before you get a strike. When you get one, however, it is worth the wait. I have pulled in many a trout and many a togue this way.

After I had learned to tie flies I used to take my kit along with me and try to duplicate many of the kinds of insects I saw the fish jump at. This kind of close study made it much easier to match colors accurately than if I sat home trying to remember what I had seen hours before. That little brownish fly you see in

June flying over the water is commonly called the mayfly. Now and then you hear people refer to it as the green drake. This lively little insect has large fan wings and an elongated body, and mixed in with the brown, a very slight greenish cast. Mayflies have two or three tails, and ten body segments. Sometimes they have only one pair of wings, but usually two—the large ones forward and the small ones to the rear.

In tying mayflies—or any others—keep the fly the approximate size of the insect you are reproducing. You can vary the hook size somewhat and tie a large fly on a small hook by getting a shank three or four inches long. But keep the fly's size as nearly exact as possible. It is easy to see that a size-eight or a size-sixteen pattern could not possibly be a good match for an insect which in life is about a size twelve.

Sometimes we took in a dance at Churchill Lake or Lac Frontiere, dancing to such up-to-the-minute tunes as "Oh! Them Golden Slippers." A few times we went to weddings, and now and then there would be a party at one cabin or another. Although we had wonderful times at these affairs, it was always pleasant to get back to our own quiet routine. At home we felt free—especially, free from the obligation of keeping up a conversation if we did not feel like talking.

Often enough Dave was asked to work with Warden Wilson at Nine Mile. Sometimes they would be gone a week at a time and I then went with the children to visit Mrs. Wilson. The camp at Nine Mile was very large. The Wilsons' cabin had three bedrooms, a large sitting room, and a kitchen, so with the men away there was plenty of room for us.

I have always admired Ruth Wilson. Like myself she spent many days alone in her camp. Unlike me, however, she was not afraid of bears, or anything else for that matter. When the men got back from their patrols, Dave and the children and I would return to our cabin to enjoy a few days together until once again Dave would have to make a trip through his district alone. Some of these were eight- or ten-day trips. Word that Dave was away got around like wildfire, and while he was out of his own district there would be a lot of illegal hunting and fishing without license. Dave always had to check up on the reports awaiting him when he returned to his own camp.

Chapter 10

Partridges, Lake Trout and Woodchucks

The partridge, which is one of the most common birds throughout this timberland, is a permanent resident and does not migrate. The sexes are quite similar in appearance, and it is only when you have read all about them that you are able to tell the male from the female. In the male, the thick black feathers on the neck are more pronounced than in the female. When the tail of the female is spread, the black band is broken in the center, while on the male this appears to be solid black.

The courtship of partridges takes place in early spring. It is also at this time that drumming by male partridges occurs and continues until late fall. When you are hunting, you will hear throughout the woods this noise, resembling thunder far off in the distance. I recall the first time Dave and I saw a partridge drumming. We'd watched the bird for an hour before we saw it drum.

The cock bird drums on the top of a fallen log. I have heard long arguments about the exact way in which the sound is produced. The partridge braces its feet and by fanning the air with great rapidity makes the drumming sound, and does not as most people think beat its wings against the side of his body. But we are tempted to believe this until we have proved it.

Partridges usually nest in May, picking out a site near the edge of a clearing or under some brush in the woods. But the nests are always hidden. The female makes a hollow in the ground, then lines it with dry leaves and feathers from her breast. I have seen nests with as many as twenty eggs, but usually they have from ten to fifteen eggs. The period of incubation is about twenty-four days. All the nesting duties and the care of the young ones are credited to the female. The food for newly hatched chicks consists of bodies of insects and green plant material. As they grow older the chicks gradually change their diet and feed on berries and small seeds. Within a few hours after partridges are hatched they are able to leave the nest and immediately follow their mother through the woods. If enemies are about, they can easily hide under leaves while the mother makes an awful fuss, flying here and there, trying to divert the attention of the enemy. I have tried many times, when I was young, to bring up a small partridge, but I have never succeeded. They will die before they will eat the food that you put in front of them. Usually partridges are not successful in outwitting predators, and too often foxes, bobcats, hawks, and even crows prey upon the family. We find that many other small animals are fond of partridges' eggs, too. And when there is a lot of rain during spring it is almost as bad. My husband most always makes away with house cats that are left in lumber camps, because he says they are destructive to small and big partridges.

There is also the spruce partridge which I have often heard called the fool hen, because of its tameness in the presence of man. You usually find them in the low land and dense spruce, fir, and tamarack swamps. They are similar to the ruffed grouse, but much smaller in size. Some people prefer them to the ruffed grouse. All the years that I remember hunting we have never once killed a spruce partridge. My idea is, as it is so tame, it would seem awful to just shoot the bird for the fun of it, especially when you can get near enough to them to almost touch them with your hand. I like to give any partridge a chance and let it fly away, then when it is at a distance from the ground, shoot as you would a flying pigeon. Our idea of hunting is not to kill all of the animals we see, but to really give them a chance to get away, or make a try to get away. This is what I call good sportsmanship. And if more hunters would do this before shooting, there would be fewer accidents. If we come upon a deer, whether it is in a clearing or the thick woods, and the deer perhaps is running, try to give a loud whistle, and you will find that eight to ten times the deer will stop and look back. Sometimes I have seen them walking toward us a good hundred feet. Deer are curious animals, and if they hear an odd noise it's sure to make them stop. It is the same with partridges.

There are many ways to cook a partridge. Dave and I prefer it best cooked in a stew. You take one or two dressed birds, thoroughly washed, and put them in a stew kettle with one quart of water. Add a small piece of salt pork, some salt and pepper, and one small onion, and let boil for two hours. Then add a few sliced potatoes. When they are nearly done, add a little thickening to the broth and let it simmer for a while longer. Dave likes dumplings in the stew, so I take one cup of flour, a pinch of salt, one teaspoonful of baking powder, and mix well with just a little water to make a thick batter. Then I add this by the spoonful to the stew and let it simmer for twenty minutes. Partridge stew is delicious this way.

Another way which is also very good is this: Boil one or more partridges in salt water until the meat is pretty well done, then add one cup of rice to every three cups of water or broth. Add, also, one can of tomatoes and one chopped onion, and let simmer for two hours. Tom Sweeney usually cooked his partridge in baked beans. He would soak the beans as usual, but add the partridge and bake it. This gives the baked beans a very different taste. Also, the breast of the partridge can be deep-fried. After dipping the breast in a beaten egg and rolling the meat in corn-meal flour, cook in deep fat as you would chickens. This is best-loved by everyone. The meat of the ruffed grouse excels the meat of the spruce partridge, which is very dark and tastes of fir gum and spruce.

Yvette, the girl we hired to take care of the children, could not learn to make a stew. Almost every day I would bring a partridge or two to our home camp and ask Yvette to make one for us. But the same thing would occur day after day. It seems all she did was to put the birds in gallons of water without salt, onions, or pork. Then she'd chuck in a few potatoes. This mess she would boil an hour or so. When we arrived tired and hungry from a long hike in the woods, there was our favorite stew—inedible. I was quite vexed those first times, but then I began joking about it and calling it Yvette stew. I just couldn't help laughing, especially when my husband dished out a plateful for himself. He would have the funniest expression on his face! When I cook a partridge stew in season now we still laugh about Yvette's efforts. Nevertheless, Yvette was a good housekeeper. She took good care of the children and she was a good cook when it came to something other than stew.

During July one year several officials came to fish, and Dave went on trips with them up into Little Pleasant Lake, Spider Lake, and many others. I stayed home for a week or so, but at the end of that time, as I was watching the last party leave for the day's fishing at Long Lake Dam, one of the men said, "Take your wife along, Dave. It's too nice to stay at the camp."

The preparations were quickly made and soon we were on our way. We planned on having fresh trout for our dinner. We landed at the dam and began to fish, but at first the fishing was not up to our expectations. I sat in the bow of our canoe, paddle in hand, watching Dave try all the techniques he knew to get us enough trout for our dinner. I noticed that he was using a dry fly which was floating well on the water. He would make a cast directly across current on a slack line and let the fly ride naturally as far as it could. Then by raising and lowering the tip of his rod he would cause the fly to bounce along the surface of the water in a wide arc until the current had swung it to a point directly below him. Retrieving it with the same irregular motion, he would pick up the fly and make a new cast, letting out more line. In this way he was able to fish a wider arc covering all the water he could comfortably reach. This method worked wonderfully, and in a few hours he had caught enough trout for our dinner.

If you have experienced the thrill of luring and landing a trout before, you will find that there are few other pleasures in life that can compare, and it is one experience you will remember for years.

Among our freshwater fish, trout is most admired for its coloration and taste. Especially trout taken in clear water. When taken in the dark, muddy bottom of lakes and ponds, trout tends to be very dark, and the flesh is nearly white in color, whereas trout taken in clear water where there is plenty of food has flesh that is a dark pink and very tasty.

It is hard to believe, but a trout's senses are highly developed; therefore, he feels the vibration of footsteps on the shore, and the reflection on the water will cause the trout to flee. But I do believe in fisherman's luck; if you read all about the habit of trout feeding, which also applies to all other fish, it will help your luck. Fish may not be always in the same place year after year and the fly that you use today may not be the right one tomorrow. If you are to become a good fisherman there are three things you must know: first, to locate the right place; second, to find the right fly; and third, to play the fly so as to resemble a living fly on the water. With enough effort, it will produce a creel of fish you will be proud of.

At Umsaskis we met a lot of people who had come up to fish. Certain ones, with special permission from the Fish and Game Department, stayed at the warden's camp, and my husband had instructions to be as helpful as possible to them. This is how we happened to meet the Smiths from Portland, a perfectly wonderful couple.

Dave and Mr. Smith decided that we would all go on a week's fishing trip together. So after taking the children to Dot Burnham's at Clayton, we packed the sleeping bags, some extra clothing, food for a week, and fishing tackle, loaded the canoe on top of our car, and headed for Churchill. We were to go to Cliff Lake, thence to Tramway and Eagle Lake. When we arrived at the wharf at Churchill, our luggage was unloaded and packed away in the canoe. The Smiths had taken along, on top of their car, a small boat for the trip to Cliff Lake. The boat, a small, heavy, flat-bottomed boat with pointed ends, had to be taken up the brook connecting Churchill and Cliff lakes, a distance of about eight miles. Mrs. Smith and I cooked a quick lunch which we all ate by the outdoor fire. Then we resumed our trip.

After we had progressed up the brook for about a mile we found that the water was very low and the boats loaded with all our luggage had to be towed—and I mean by hand. The black flies became so terrible that no dope could possibly keep them away. With the heat of the afternoon sun, the black flies, and water to our ankles, the trip was made all the more interesting.

At the first abandoned camp we came to at the edge of the brook, Dave found a couple of old pails in which he made a smudge. He told us to carry them along to keep the flies away. Everyone was exhausted when we arrived at the outlet of Cliff Lake. As with most lakes in this region, there was a dam at one end. This meant that all the luggage, including the canoe and the boat, had to be carried over the dam and reloaded again to be paddled to our destination, which was not too far away at the head of the lake.

The road to paradise is said to be a difficult one—and that can certainly be said of the road to the fisherman's paradise we now found ourselves upon. Once there, however, all agreed that it was worth all the fly bites and sore muscles. We found another abandoned camp and decided to settle in the cook room. There were shelves on the wall and a large table and, at one end of the room, the place where, years before, a huge cookstove had stood. As we found it, it was hardly the kind of camp fishermen dream of when they look over the booklets sent out by the State Publicity Bureau.

The Smiths beamed when Dave suggested that they go out in the canoe and catch enough trout for supper. And while they fished he and I prepared the place for the night. Dave went into the woods and cut down a dozen or more cedar boughs and a five-foot pole which would serve as a broomstick. With a length of wire he fastened the boughs securely to one end of the stick, thus making a fairly effective broom. With this I did a good thorough job of sweeping the floor of the old camp. As in most abandoned camps, there were loads of porcupine leavings. These had to be cleaned out before anyone could set up beds or go about cooking. The broom swept clean and left behind a pleasant scent of cedar. Dave found some boards and with his ax and some nails knocked together a table out of doors. Dave always takes along in his lunch box a large piece of oilcloth which we spread on the table. Then he built a fireplace with rocks just by the door in front of the camp. Before long we had it as clean as a whistle and homey enough to satisfy anyone.

When the Smiths returned everything was shipshape. They came back with a good batch of trout, but their surprise and pleasure at seeing what we had accomplished during their absence was, I think, just as intense as their pride in their catch. We had potatoes boiling, and the aroma of coffee filled the air. That was a good evening, one of the especially nice things about it being the fun we had just sitting around relaxing in front of the outdoor fireplace, talking about a hundred things of common interest. I always feel that friendly rambling conversation at the end of a busy day is one of the nicest things life has to offer.

The next few days we spent fishing and exploring the woods and hills and trails around Cliff Lake. The fishing there was wonderful. We trolled for togue and trout and caught all we could use of both. The togue here had flesh a deep pink which reminded us of saltwater salmon. They were very fat and tasty. I recall that we also hooked into an occasional whitefish, which ran a good pound or more. Some sportsmen sniff at bait fishing, but I have seen my husband catch togue and trout using almost anything for bait. At Cliff Lake, with hooks baited with salt pork, he pulled in a good fat togue and a large trout.

This was my first trip to Cliff Lake, and as always when I visit new places I spent a lot of time exploring. The lake itself is not very large—about two miles long and a half-mile wide. I found that the surrounding timber had been well cut down by the company which had operated in the area. Deer were plentiful in the vicinity. During one of our walks, Dave explained to us that deer soon exhaust the feed in the forest and seek places where grass grows.

The deer population, he said, changes and shifts from time to time. Although in this general area they are never so scarce as to fail to lure hunters. Here in this lumbering country the deer follow the ax. It always used to hurt me at heart to see the forest being cut down, but after I learned the ways of the forest I realized that the cutting down of the trees was frequently a good thing. If a forest is let alone by man, Dave explained, and manages to escape the menaces of wind, fire, pest, and disease, its individual trees mature, die, and fall without serving any purpose other than enhancing the landscape. A forest, then, to serve man best must be cut. While the lumber company did not intend to do so, they have helped the deer population by giving them patches of clear area which furnished green patches of grass which resulted from the exposure.

We are not mistaken when we believe that in the forest deer are all over the place.

While all of these matters are the concern of the game warden, his chief function is to regulate and supervise and limit the inroads men make on the fish and game population. In recent years improved firearms and fishing tackle have been responsible for more game and fish being taken annually. Improved transportation facilities, modern cars, an extensive system of improved roads, and airplanes equipped to put down on our remote lakes, permit hunters and fishermen to go farther into the woods and lakes more and more.

After this interesting walk we returned to camp, for it was past supper time. However, we had seen a good many places of interest and had had a good lesson in woods lore. None of us minded the late supper that night.

The hours and days of our trip went by very fast, and soon it was time to return to Umsaskis. The trip was made much more easily than the one out. Although the boat and canoe had to be hauled part of the way, they followed the current down much more readily. Once we got to Umsaskis the Smiths bade us good-bye, thanked us for a wonderful time, and promised to come again.

One afternoon, Tom Sweeney came by and we fell into conversation. I told him how I would love to have a woodchuck, for they make wonderful pets, far better than cats. I told him of the time my brother Lionel had picked up a very tiny one only a few hours old. Returning from a trip to Seven Islands over on the upper St. John, he came across a family of woodchucks. The mother had evidently been disturbed in her nest, for she was moving her young ones to a different place. When she saw Lionel coming she dropped the little one she was carrying. My brother picked it up and decided to keep it. Its eyes were still closed and it could not walk. Lionel put it in his shirt pocket and continued toward home. There were many ohs and ahs when he brought it into our house. I remember how we fed the baby woodchuck with an eye dropper. In a few days its eyes opened and it became very active and tame—a real house pet. We kept it all through the summer and fall. One day Father took it to Clayton so it could nest for the winter, for woodchucks hibernate like bears.

Tom had told me there were several of them in the clearing near his cabin. At that time Toma Nicholas, who was known throughout the area as Indian Tom, was visiting Tom for a few days. I presume Tom told the Indian of my wish, for the next day Toma appeared at my door with a burlap bag in his hand. I thought maybe they were out of potatoes and he wanted to borrow some for supper. But still, the bag looked heavy. Suddenly I noticed something moving in it. I kept looking at Toma and the burlap bag in his hand, waiting for him to speak, but not a word came out of him. Toma was a wily, tough, severe-looking old

Indian. Many years before he had killed a bear in a hand-to-hand fight and his face still bore the scars of that battle. To tell the truth I was—in a way that is hard to explain—afraid of him.

Nevertheless I said, "Come on in, Toma, and sit down."

He said, "No, thank you," and at the same time shoved the bag into my hand, adding, "You wanted a woodchuck, didn't you?"

I looked in the bag and saw that there was a full-sized wood-chuck in it. I couldn't help smiling. "This is a big one, Toma. I wanted a kitten. I could never train this. How in the world did you ever catch hold of such a big one?"

I handed the bag with the woodchuck in it back to Indian Tom. The old man was so disappointed that he just said, "Oh," turned on his heel, and started to walk rapidly back along the path to Tom's cabin. I hadn't meant to offend him, but I am afraid I did. I had no idea he would be so earnest about it.

One day Arlene and Robert said they wanted to hold a moose bird in their hands. Moose birds, or Canadian jays, are not at all timid. I went to the garage and after rummaging around found a wooden box with a cover on it. I carried the box over to the table on the porch, fastened one end of a long string to the cover, and then put some food in the box. After that I placed the box on the ground a few yards in front of our cabin, and after propping up the cover, led the string in through one of the front windows of the cabin. Arlene and Robert and I then sat in the living room and waited until some moose birds fluttered down to examine the box. Presently one of them hopped into the box to get at the food I had placed in it. I pulled the string, the cover fell down, and we had captured our first bird.

The children were dancing with joy. With a glove on my right hand I reached in and got hold of the moose bird. It acted very calm, didn't peck at me at all, and as it turned out, I didn't even need gloves. We kept it for several hours and then released it. We repeated this harmless trapping over and over. Sometimes we caught little winter birds, sometimes squirrels.

Dave came home one time as we were waiting to make a capture. To help us out and to make it easier to pull the string freely, he bored a little hole in the window sash. Thereafter we had much greater success.

During the month of August when the black flies and mosquitoes were not so bad we made a trip to Cliff Brook, which runs down from Cliff Lake into Churchill Lake. Blanchette's lumber camp was in that area and my husband, who so often had to make a check on such camps, decided this time to take the children and me along. So I packed up all we required for such a trip. Food was put in the lunch box which Dave always carries in the canoe. We took our tent, two sleeping bags, towels, and soap, which I put in a small kettle, and some cookies which I stored in another kettle in case the children wanted to munch on the way. Then the canoe was loaded on top of the car and early one morning we left. Bobby, who was always so full of energy, was very quiet now, much impressed by this, his first camping trip. When we arrived at Churchill Lake everything was unloaded at the wharf and placed in the canoe for our trip up to Cliff Brook, less than ten miles away. The water was very smooth and of so deep a blue that we could see our reflections as we paddled over it. We caught enough trout for our dinner and then poled up the brook a couple of miles. Dave picked out a beautiful place to set up our tent. Then we carried our luggage to the spot where the tent was to be pitched and I set about my chores while Dave went to cut some fir boughs for our beds.

In our haste to get everything ready in good time we didn't notice little Arlene carrying the kettle in which I had stored the soap and towels. Unable to tell which was which, she had taken that kettle instead of the cookie kettle. Both she and Bobby must have been getting hungry, for there she was with Bobby following her, bumping his head on the kettle that Arlene was carrying. They were having a most wonderful time when suddenly Arlene discovered she had been carrying the wrong pail and burst into tears. She soon got over it and everything was fine.

After supper Dave made up the beds, using the fir boughs he had gathered. The children slept in one sleeping bag, we in the other. The bags were as comfy as our own bed back home and the children were sound asleep a minute after they were tucked in. It had been a busy day and we were all tired out.

Before turning in for the night Dave and I went for a swim. We found this very refreshing after our hard day. The water was so warm and relaxing! Then we sat before the fire for a while, talking softly. The sky was filled with stars that night and the moon was reflected so brilliantly on the water in front of us that we could see the surrounding ridges. The ripples on the water looked like silver lace mixed with a very little black. Once in a while if we were very quiet we heard the whistle of a deer back in the timberland or the hoot of an owl close by, and occasionally the thumping of a snowshoe rabbit.

I could tell by the expression on his face that Dave was very happy to have his family with him. He is not one to speak of his joy or his sorrow, but if you know him you learn to read his eyes as readily as you read a book. My husband is five feet nine and weighs about a hundred and sixty-five pounds. He is slim, has brown eyes and hair, and delicate features. Like all woodsmen his complexion is reddish from constant exposure to sun, wind, rain, and cold. No matter where you see him he is always neat. He has the manners of a gentleman. He never argues or brags of his work or the things he has done. He never says anything but good of anyone. Yet he is not a prude or a softy. It is just that he combines normal, healthy, active male interests with a gentle, sensitive, good heart. Because of my French-Canadian background, he loves to tease me with French-Canadian dialect stories. Around the campfire at night, Dave, a good storyteller, is at his best. He has a wealth of interesting personal experiences and factual information to draw on, and he is one of the best reciters of narrative poetry I have ever listened to. With no effort at all he can recite the endless verses of poems like "The Cremation of Sam McGee" and "Dangerous Dan McGrew."

After breakfast the next day, Dave left us at the tent while he went in to Blanchette's camp which was six miles away. He told us he would be gone for about three hours, so the children and I settled for the day. With a jackknife, which I always carry in my pocket on a trip, I began to whittle little guns and canoes for Bobby. I kept a small fire going in the fireplace and when dinner time came I cooked over the open fire. I had brought along a jar of hamburger that I had put up for such occasions, and I boiled some potatoes and carrots. It sounds simple enough but it was a feast to eat there in front of the fireplace. The children and I had ravenous out-of-doors appetites.

I have often watched the lumbermen eating in the open. Their appetites are so great it makes you hungry just to watch them. More than once Dave and I have arrived at a lumber camp just at dinner time, and we have always appreciated the courtesy of the woodsmen who so readily and so generously shared their food with us. Nothing else but we must eat. They simply wouldn't let us refuse.

I looked at my watch and thought that Dave should soon be back. We began watching in the direction he had gone, but to our surprise he returned from an altogether different direction on the opposite side of the brook. After a cup of tea and a cookie, we spent the remainder of the afternoon around the campfire. An hour before dark we went fishing for trout for our breakfast and when we returned, put the children to bed.

The next morning as we packed up it was very cloudy and the wind was blowing hard. It looked very much like rain as the clouds were rushing across the sky. By the time we were ready to go a light mist was falling and the wind was coming in gusts. Our passage down the brook was short and relatively calm. However, when we arrived at the mouth of the brook and got a look out over the lake, it was an altogether different story. The whitecaps were huge and some of the waves were fifteen feet high. It was impossible to go any farther. An attempt to cross Churchill Lake under such conditions would have been suicidal.

I had never been wind-bound before, but as long as we were all together it seemed to me it would not be so terrible. We had to get under cover so Dave pitched our tent near the edge of the woods. Later we had a cold lunch. Then the children took their nap as if everything were normal. As the afternoon wore on the wind slowed down a bit and the water began to calm. At five we had another cold lunch, for we didn't dare make a fire with the wind still blowing. The mist stopped falling.

By eight o'clock that evening we decided that it was safe enough to move on. We reloaded our canoe, putting the children in the middle and spreading the tent over them to keep them from getting wet from the spray. I sat in the bow so I could now and then reach under the tent which covered them and hold their hands, letting them know I was still there. They could not see, for their little heads were covered up. The lake was still stirring up some pretty large waves, but we managed to reach the wharf at Churchill just as darkness fell. It had been a wonderful, exciting trip.

Chapter 11

The Family Grows Again

During summer there were many parties of fishermen and jodmy husband was kept very busy. He had, of course, to continue his night patrols all through summer and fall. Nevertheless, he took me along on a good many one-day trips and night patrols. With only a young girl looking after the children, we didn't feel like leaving them alone too long at a time. Little Arlene was quite a girl now and Bobby was creeping and very noisy. We just couldn't keep him on the porch, so I made him three pairs of overalls with padded knees and little cotton mittens and we let him play in the sand, where he would have the grandest time creeping back and forth on his hands and knees. One day he crept away unnoticed. I had gone into the cabin to get a book to read while he was playing outside, and when I came out there was no Bobby in sight. I decided that he might have set off in the direction Dave had taken a while earlier and sure enough, there he was at Willie's camp. He had gone there all the way on his hands and knees. We often wondered why he was so full of energy and yet was so slow to walk. He didn't walk until he was fourteen months old.

Almost before we knew it, we received a fair warning from Tom on his return trip from fishing at the head of Umsaskis that the raspberries were ripe in clearances on the old landing and we best be gathering all we could for canning. I have seen Maman Pacquet put away as many as a hundred gallons of raspberries at one time. Her family was large, she frequently had company during the winter, and Maman was determined not to be caught short. My thirty quarts seemed like a spoonful next to her huge supply.

During the month of July we used to take a day off to go to Lac Frontiere to buy what strawberries we needed for our winter's canning. We also went in August to buy honey. We scouted several towns at first and finally settled on a place in Daaquam where the honey was of the best quality. I recall the big roll of money the old gent who sold the honey had in his pocket. Perhaps they were all one-dollar bills; nevertheless, his smooth, fat roll, more than three inches in diameter, was the biggest and most impressive I have ever seen. You could tell by the expression on his face that he loved to take it out. He would pat it with great contentment as he added to it the money he had just been given for the honey he had sold. We have often wondered if this was his whole life's savings.

The honey man had a nice farm, a good house, and a grown, married family. After a couple of years of honey purchasing we got to know each other well and his wife always had tea for us. One further reason why we liked them was that they both admired our children.

After buying a supply of honey, we always had a feast and invited Uncle Will Gardner and Tom Sweeney for supper. Tom still hadn't taught me his way of baking biscuits and I had the feeling he had put off showing me how because he liked to bake them himself. I enjoyed watching him fuss about the kitchen making a big thing of the biscuit making, so I let him prepare them by himself. Besides, I must admit, his biscuits were delicious with honey.

Late one autumn day as we chugged across Beau Lake, way up on the Canadian border, Dave shouted to me above the racket of the outboard and pointed skyward. There, streaming southward, was a flight of ducks which must have numbered several hundred. It was a beautiful sight, thrilling in a strange kind of way. The thought of these wild birds so obediently heeding their instinct and setting out on a flight which would lead them to feeding grounds thousands of miles away was somehow awesome.

Our appreciation of the beauty of the flight did not, however, deter Dave and me from making up our minds that it was about time we did some duck hunting. I had never done any, and strangely enough, neither had Dave. Before the week was out we had bought a good duck gun, some decoys, a duck call, and some other necessary equipment. Then, on the first day of the season, we bought our duck stamp and early the following morning, before sunup, set out on our first hunt.

The wind on the lake was blowing a gale that morning, and we discovered after a half-hour of fussing with the decoys in the choppy water that unless the weather calmed we were going to be out of luck, for the decoys were constantly being upended and flipped over by the wind and the waves. Decoys on the water are supposed to look like the real thing to ducks flying overhead. But the crazy actions of our decoys would have been enough to scare any overhead flock into a quick retreat. We knuckled under to the weather that day and chalked it up to experience.

A few days later Dave and I set out again and accomplished nothing in our early-morning quest. Later on in the day, paddling back from a lumber camp which we had visited, we decided to scout around the lake. I took the shotgun from its case, got out some shells, and settled back, trying to be alert and relaxed at the same time. Dave paddled slowly from one grassy point to another, following the shore of the lake as closely as possible.

Suddenly Dave whispered to me and pointed his paddle toward a little island not far from the shore. There on a floating log a little offshore from the island, a half-dozen ducks sat prettying themselves. In a low whisper Dave suggested that he would let me out of the canoe on the far side of the island and then paddle to the mainland shore. That way I might get a chance to get a good shot at the ducks when they took to the air. After I had fired he would come back to the island to pick me up.

With great difficulty I did just what he suggested. The little island was dense with undergrowth and dead logs and extremely muddy. Trying to work my way quietly through this tangle, I got myself thoroughly smeared. I had mud all over my arms and legs and face and hair. But I didn't mind, for I was succeeding in working my way to a point from which I could get a good shot at the ducks when they took off. And I was just about at this point when, for some reason that we have never been able to determine, Dave, on the opposite side of the little island, made a loud swishing noise with his paddle and the ducks, alarmed, started to quack warnings to one another. And in another minute, with a great flapping of wings they were gone.

I didn't get a chance to get a shot at them. I did, however, get a chance to give Dave a piece of my mind when, a moment later, he paddled around the point of the island to pick me up. My bedraggled, mud-sopped condition didn't seem nearly as amusing to me as it did to him. But we made it up. On our way back I brought down two fat ones and we had broiled duck for supper after all.

A new addition to our camp was being built. With the help of Tom and some of the boys Dave knew, good progress was being made and it would soon be finished. We had by now decided to use it for a kitchen and looked forward eagerly to the extra space we would gain by the addition of this extra room.

By September we were settled in our new kitchen, and I am proud of the work Dave and I did. We painted the floor gray and Tom built a corner cupboard in the left-hand corner as we entered the kitchen. Under the window facing the lake he built a sideboard, and next to it placed the cookstove. A door opens at the other end of the kitchen where we can see as far down the lake as the thoroughfare. New white ruffled curtains and a new tablecloth make it look very inviting.

Through the open window on this September day I could feel the cool air of an early fall. While I served our midday lunch we could see the bright coloring of the hardwood trees on the ridge across the lake, and you felt a warning that winter would soon be here. Next thing you know, bright and early on an autumn morning you are outside your cabin with the cross-cut saw on your shoulder and an ax in your hand, and off you go looking for some good sound trees. Four or five days' cutting and chopping and splitting gives you a good start for the coming winter. This year, we didn't need so much camp wood, because a new member of the family was expected to arrive some time in December and I would be moving out for a few months. We had decided to rent an apartment at Lac Frontiere. During this time Dave would be checking the timber crews as before and following the cuttings, checking the many lumber camps he had in his district.

Despite the expected arrival of a new baby, I managed to do a little bird hunting along the road. This didn't require too much walking. Deer hunting, which involved fairly rough hiking, was of course out of the question.

We were happy at the thought of having another baby. Arlene would just turn two around the time of the new baby's arrival, but we liked having our babies so nearly of one age. It meant a little more work but a lot more fun for us and it meant much in added companionship for the children.

In the middle of November we moved. Dave had found us a nice furnished apartment in a two-family house. Our baby, a little girl, was born the second of December. Dave had just come home for a day when she arrived. Everything went well. She was a little darling, as fat and pink as a cherub. We decided to call her Hilda.

Warden Wilson was also left alone at Nine Mile while his wife moved to Jackman for the same reason I moved. In December she gave birth to a pair of twins.

For a month Dave, who was working with Warden Wilson, managed to be with us every two or three days. I enjoyed that winter at Lac Frontiere, because my family had lived there when we weren't at Seven Islands. All my girlhood friends lived there and we visited each other very often. I had a woman who came every morning to do the housework and the baby's wash so I could devote most of each day to the three children.

In March, shortly before Easter, we returned to Umsaskis Lake. Our home camp looked very good to me. The snow was melting fast, although the ice was still very thick on the lakes and would last at least until the end of April. Just before the ice goes out in the spring it turns different colors. At first it is a bright blue, almost a pale blue, when the sun shines. Then after a while the ice becomes grayish with patches of white. It seems then as though the ice has risen like a cake. Then of a sudden the ice gets very dark, almost black, and very brittle. At this stage it is very dangerous to travel on it. On some occasions I have seen men crossing the ice carrying with them a ten- or twelve-foot pole in case they should break through. Even so they are taking chances.

If the wind blows hard when the ice is at that stage, in no time the ice breaks up and the lake is soon clear water. But if we have no wind the ice lasts much longer and finally melts away. This happens only on rare occasions, for during the breakup spell the weather is mostly cold during the forenoon and very warm in the afternoon. There is, too, a lot of rain and high wind.

I liked to watch the trees budding and the little spears of early grass which would all of a sudden be standing there bravely in front of the door one morning long before the countryside as a whole started to turn green. It was thrilling to watch the swallows returning from their long winter in the south and to hear the ducks quacking over the blue water. The ducks appear to be as happy to be back as we are to have them back. They immediately begin to choose mates and to build nests.

After the March rains it began to look like spring, for the snow was melting fast and the appearance of the ice was beginning to change in places, though of course it was still solid. Early as it was, my thoughts began to turn toward fly-casting, and more than ever I was anxious to tag along with Dave on his trips through his district. His canoe had been repaired and his outboard motor overhauled. I was ready too. My spring cleaning was over. I had hung new curtains on the windows, and laid a new carpet on our floor. Since we now had three children, we had had to convert the new kitchen into a bedroom. We were using our first camp as a kitchen and sitting room. The addition of a day bed and a few bright pillows gave this room a nice cozy look.

In the middle of April Dave went to the hospital in Quebec to have an operation. I had to stay home with the children. Our neighbor Tom came every day to help with the wood and the water, but I was pretty blue. I hated not being able to go with Dave and I hated not knowing how serious his condition was.

I did a lot of sewing to occupy myself and to keep myself from brooding. A few days before my husband was to leave the hospital I packed up the few things we needed and called Charlie Hafford, the mailman, to come after the children and me so that we could go to Lac Frontiere to meet Dave there as he came through on his way back. In the afternoon we went to the main road to meet Charlie. Tom was going to look after our camp while I was away.

At Lac Frontiere we stayed with Charlie's wife. On April the twentieth, having gotten word from the hospital that Dave had been discharged and was on his way home, we went to the station to meet him. He did not expect us and the meeting was a pleasant surprise for him. His operation had been successful, although he looked very thin. The important thing was that he was much better. We stayed a few days with Charlie and his wife Theresa. Then we returned to Umsaskis Lake, and under orders from his doctor Dave took a month off to rest.

As soon as Dave's month's rest was up, he set out on a trip to Ross Lake. Dave isn't one to stay put. Therefore, after gathering a few things he needed for his trip he was off for a few days. It was a beautiful day and the scenery now was wonderfully mild and placid. I think just then its beauties grew on me and made me love this wilderness even more the longer I lived here. I promised myself that while the children were napping, I would take a walk on one of my favorite trails.

Except for my trip to Lac Frontiere I had not, during the past month, ventured more than twenty yards from our camp. The next day proved to be warm and sunny again, so while the children were napping I wandered into one of the trails I like so well. The foliage was as green as ever, the tall trees were standing as quietly as if no one had intruded there throughout the last two generations. I ventured into an open space and a company of crows were holding a meeting. Apparently I must have insulted them for they began to caw-caw-caw, and took flight to securer solitude. I thought I was probably the first human shape they had seen in months.

However, their voices were in accord with the influence of a quiet, sunny, warm afternoon. They were so far now above my head that I could hardly see them; if they were cawing yet, I could not hear them anymore.

When I returned, Tom Sweeney was sitting on the steps smoking his favorite pipe. Tom is a keen observer of nature which we suspect is almost as rare a character as an original poet. And nature in return for his love showed him secrets which few others are permitted to witness. He is familiar with animals and fish and fowl and reptiles and he had many strange stories to tell of his adventures. He is familiar with herbs and flowers wherever they grew. He has learned what can be used for medicine, and what cannot be used. He is also on intimate terms with the clouds and can foretell the changes in weather. Tom will give you the true image of what he saw, just as a lake reflects its wooded banks, showing every leaf, yet giving the wild beauty of the whole.

At about five Tom took his leave and with an occasional glance at the beautiful sunset, I went about getting the children some supper. I fed them, played a little game with them, and soon put them to bed. Then I settled down to read a book while the radio played. I turned in soon after ten and shortly dropped off to sleep, wondering how Dave was withstanding the trip to Ross Lake.

He returned the next day not too worn out, saying that he'd had a good trip. Outboard motoring had been excellent, for the water at this time of the year was still quite high in the streams. The next few days were spent checking between Clayton Lake and Churchill Lake. I'd pack up the baby's formula and a few things for the children, and all of us would accompany Dave on these trips. Some days we went as far as Nine Mile. I stayed there many times while Dave worked with Warden Wilson. This gave me the opportunity to visit with Wilson's wife Ruth for several days. It was not too often I had a chance to converse with a woman, and to my dismay I found that I was at a loss, used as I was to the conversation of only woodsmen, trappers, and guides. Speaking of clothes seemed useless to me, for I wore only jodhpurs and slacks and on rare occasions, a dress. I seldom wanted to talk of our children, for I know that a lot of women dislike talking about babies. Each mother is a law unto herself insofar as the ways of feeding, caring for, and bringing up children are concerned.

The first to come to Umsaskis after the winter was over was Levi Dow. We loved to see Levi, for with him came all the news. Besides, he was a great storyteller and joked most of the time. His voice and his laugh, so loud and jolly, were unforgettable.

He came in this day saying, "Are you going to have another baby this year, Annette? You've got three now. I should think you've had enough."

All I could say was, "Time will tell. And at that I wouldn't mind having a dozen. You know I have an aunt who had twenty-four kids."

This was greeted with a great laugh.

Chapter 12
Old-Timers

U ncle Will Gardner and Willie Mills—the fire wardens at Umsaskis Lake—and Tom Sweeney made a great trio talking about old times and of their young days. As a game warden's wife I came in contact with very few women. But I met many men on the numerous trips I took with Dave through the woods, summer and winter. In many cases we slept and ate in lumber camps. By the end of my first three years I had learned all about the woodsmen's way of life, their interests, and their work. I got to know all about logs and pulp cuttings and timber driving. I got to know the names of each of the jobbers at different camps and the locations of the camps. I knew the clerks and cooks and scalers. I listened to the trappers telling Dave of their troubles and of their experiences catching and outwitting animals. I listened to guides tell of their troubles, too: low water, poor fishing, poor pay, motor trouble, leaky canoes, and short rations.

I enjoyed sitting and listening to these old-timers, since I was always interested in everything concerning the woods. The major conversation among the three of them was of the happenings during the previous winter. Uncle Will and Willie Mills, who arrived on the job in late spring, needed to be caught up. Willie also was always full of talk about his sister's wonderful cooking and some of her recipes which he had brought along. But this enthusiasm and his interest in fancy cooking soon died out and he was back again on the simple diet which seemed to please him and Uncle Will best.

This consisted of hot biscuits, boiled potatoes, fried salt pork, and once in a while, molasses gingerbread. To sit there and watch them eat, one would think it was the best meal ever put on a table. After they had worked hard all day long their appetites were ravenous.

Uncle Will, who was in his late sixties, worked every day, ate hugely, and looked fine. His complexion was clear, his hair only slightly grayed. He was a big man weighing one hundred and eighty pounds and standing five feet eleven inches. At one time he had poled a canoe fifty miles in one day.

I recall that the first year I was married I wanted to knit a pair of stockings for Dave as a surprise. To my disappointment, after I had the leg knitted I couldn't continue, for the simple reason that I could not knit the heel. So when Uncle Will dropped by one day for a minute's chat, I told him of my problem. He laughed, saying, "I'll show you. I've knitted many a sock in my day."

So I have the distinction of being one of the few women in the world who was taught to knit stockings by a man. Furthermore, Uncle Will taught me well and I remember with some embarrassment that he made me unravel much of what I had already knitted as it was too small. Since that day I have always knitted for my family, and Dave praises his warm woolen stockings every time he puts them on.

Often enough Uncle Will sang for us. He was a good singer but he sang songs that no one remembers today, songs of many, many years ago. One of them began like this:

1.
My name is Howard Kerry.
At Grand Falls I was born
In a quiet little cottage
By the banks of the St. John,

Where small birds chant their note so true
And the tumbling waters roar
And ivy vines so thickly twine
Around the cottage by the shore.

2.
The day I left my happy home
Mother took me by the hand.
Don't forget your parents, child,
While in a faraway land.
Mother led me to a seat
Beneath the willow tree.
With quivering lips, my boy sit down,
I want to talk with thee.

3.
Look back to yonder hillside, boy.
The grass is green.
Roses and violets, wildflowers can be seen;
Fragrant flowers numberless,
Of every shade and hue,
Sparkling in the sunlight ray
All wet with morning dew.

4.
The dewdrops sparkle in the sun.
Like diamonds rich and rare.
The odor most beautiful
Sweet doth perfume the air.
Flowers are most beautiful,
Attracting to the eye.
Remember 'neath their colors
The serpent there does lie.

5.
When you are in a strange land
And faraway land I'll have you
Beware of each pleasure and its poison . . .

And this would go on for fifteen or twenty more verses.

One evening at one of these gatherings Uncle Will, Tom, and Dave and I got to talking about the Fish and Game Department and its origin. The department itself gave out very little information about its origin and methods of law enforcement. It was our impression, however, that it had started not many years before in the southern part of the state and gradually spread its influence and authority up into the backwoods.

Oncle Gus had been a game warden in this very same district back in the days when the forest was virtually untouched by the tracks of hunters or fishermen or poachers. That was long ago, in 1904, when birch-bark canoes and pirogues were still being used and the only road up in this area was the California Road. There was, of course, a scattering of people who had settled throughout the timberland.

The road I am talking about was established in 1750 and given the name California Road many years later. It started at a little village on the shore of the St. Lawrence River in Quebec Province. It ran southwest to the watershed of the Big Black River, on to Depot Lake, through Caron Farm and Seven Islands, across the St. John River to Long Lake, and across at the outlet; thence to Musquacook Lake, to Ashland and Houlton, and from there to Augusta. In the old days this road provided one of the few land links in this region between Canada and the United States. The name "California Road" had a special meaning for people back in the middle of the nineteenth century, because the road covered a distance of three hundred and fifty miles, a stretch long enough to bring faraway California to mind.

Years later, a man by the name of White came to the Seven Islands area, established himself on the shores of the St. John River, cleared an acre of land, and began to cultivate it. He is said to have been the first one to apply the name Seven Islands to this place, there being seven large islands within an area of about three miles. White lived at Seven Islands only a short while. However, the place remained much as he had left it, and a man named Carry moved in when White departed and took over White's holding. White's Point, as Carry named the place, was, many years later, used as a graveyard for men who had died during lumbering.

Later on Carry built a place a mile or so farther up the St. John River. He cleared more land to cultivate and began to cut down lumber which was at that time hewn on four sides and hauled by oxen to the riverbank. Then during the spring freshets it was floated down the river to St. John, New Brunswick, and shipped from there to all parts of the world.

There is a story that back in 1822, William Belanger, a thirteen-year-old boy from St-Pamphile, Quebec, was sent by this man Carry from Seven Islands to Ashland to fetch an ox for breeding purposes. The round trip via the California Road was over seventy miles and young Belanger completed the trip in two weeks.

As the years passed by, many people took homesteads at Seven Islands and along the California Road. In those days lumbering was their only source of livelihood, and as lumbering progressed and more and more people moved in, a game warden was sent to this part of the wilderness. This was Ben Woodward, who came to live here in 1902 and stayed until 1908. He was replaced by Bert Spencer. By then the idea of a game warden was generally accepted and people began to pay some attention to Spencer's orders and suggestions. He issued the first trapping licenses to several men who started trapping here. They cost five dollars then as they do today. In unorganized townships, hunting and fishing licenses were sold for twenty-five cents. The game warden himself was permitted to trap while on duty if he wished.

In 1917, Bert Spencer resigned from the service and was then employed as a caretaker at Long Lake Dam. He was a great guy who in his day as game warden had had hard country and difficult people to contend with. In those days people lived on whatever moose or deer they could kill. And such folks, used to the freedom of the timberland, gave Bert a hard time when he tried to get them to abide by the new fish and game laws.

Ernest Spinny was next. He built a camp three miles from Seven Islands for himself and his wife and two daughters. Warden Spinny traveled on foot through this whole large area, going as far as Baker Lake at the head of the St. John River. He built shelters here and there where night overtook him, and a number of small camps throughout his district. Through him there was much more law enforcement since lumbering was going on on a big scale and many more people had moved in. Trappers were more numerous also. Deer abounded in great number, but the caribou, once so plentiful, had disappeared and moose were very scarce.

Ernest remained at Seven Islands patrolling the St. John River as far as Baker Lake. Law enforcement was by then in full swing. Killed deer were reported as a matter of routine and the opening and closing dates of hunting and fishing seasons were widely publicized. By that time the Lacroix Company had purchased Seven Islands, which was very large. The company's operations went as far as the Clayton Lake area. Over the course of years several smaller companies which had been engaged in cutting fir and spruce logs went out of business or moved to other areas. In 1923, the Lacroix Company built a road beginning at Lac Frontiere and extending as far as Churchill Lake. It was completed in 1926, for men were coming in by the hundreds for the pulp cutting. After so many years of rest the timberland was rich again.

Charley Green was the first chief game warden we ever met. He was no stranger to the area, for he had been up here in 1926 to help Spinny build a large camp nine miles from Seven Islands. After all these years the name remains as such, Nine Mile. It is a cheerful location right on the bank of the St. John River, lined all along with silver birch. It was at this point, a little above the camp, that a ferry crossing was made. The ferryboat was fastened to a wire stretched across the river and with the help of the current and a strong pair of arms you could work your way across.

It was here also that in later years the company built a bridge which appropriately enough was called Nine Mile Bridge. This also served as the title of Helen Hamlin's book, a very entertaining account of her experiences in the area. The Spinny camp became her home during the time she lived in that part of the woods during the '40s with her game-warden husband.

In 1924, Henry Taylor was appointed to serve in the Allagash area. He was the first game warden to cover that part of the wilderness since 1910. Henry lived in a little camp on the shore of Umsaskis Lake with his wife and child. For two years he worked through that area and then resigned from the service. Jack Gardner from the Allagash replaced him and was located there for two years. By then the Lacroix Company had begun to operate in that section of the country. In 1928, when Dave was hired, he received orders to start work immediately at Umsaskis Lake. Reporting to the chief warden, he was given a canvas canoe and a Johnson motor and told to work with Warden

Gardner. The plan was for Gardner to be transferred to another Allagash district and for Dave, after a breaking-in period, to take over this one.

Dave knew this part of the wilderness because he had in previous years worked as a surveyor for the International Paper Company. But as far as canvas canoe and outboard motor were concerned, that was all new to him. He was used only to poling and bateaus. But in his willingness to learn, he made up for his inexperience and before long became an expert. I have on many occasions been told that my husband is one of the best canoemen in the state. The children and I feel very proud of him.

Dave's appointment came at a time when more than thirty-five hundred men were working in the pulp operation. The Lacroix Company was at its busiest. Many of these lumbermen were French-Canadian, men who liked to fish, trap, and hunt whether it was open season or not. They were ignorant of all game laws, and it was Dave's job to explain the rules and regulations to them. None of them could read English, so of what use was the fish and game law book to them?

Dave spent a great many days following the lumber camps, in winter on snowshoes, during the summer by water and on foot, and to a limited extent by car. Permits to pass over the company road were issued to fishermen and hunters in the fall. Hunting was at its best then, and in a twenty-mile drive along the road one would spot forty or fifty deer and a great many partridges. Night patrols were ordered all over the district, for the night hunters were many.

By 1930, Commissioner George Stobie had effected so many changes that the wardens in the area had increased by 100 percent. He also issued uniforms to all wardens. These were of a dark-gray flannel cloth which was far from being tough enough to withstand the rough going of trips through the woods. In

1933, a different uniform was issued, more durable and in much better taste. Their steel-gray breeches had a bright-red stripe running down the seams. They were worn with a gray shirt and black tie. There were also a trim tunic and Sam Browne belt and a good-looking gray hat. Four years later still another uniform was issued. This time the trousers were powder blue with a black stripe. They were worn with a blue shirt with black trimmings and topped off by an Eisenhower-type jacket and blue cap. A bright red coat was issued for fall use and a blue dress coat for winter. To my mind this last uniform was the best.

Chapter 13

Tramway

One August I went on a trip to Tramway with Dave. We got a housekeeper to look after the children while we were gone and arranged for Tom to stop in each day and see that they were getting along all right. While we were putting things together for our trip, Dave suggested that he had better take a look at a bear trap he had set a few days before. Sure enough the trap was sprung, but what Dave had caught was a three-month-old bear cub. Although to some it might have seemed cruel, Dave did away with the cub. Little bears are cute, but big ones, as we had discovered, are a menace. Dave's theory that little bears grow to be big ones was hard to argue against. Result: one dead bear cub.

The next day we left for the Tramway area, stopping along the way to check fishing parties here and there. We finally arrived at Camp Parson which Bert Duty had occupied for many years, spent the night there, and early the next morning headed once again for the Tramway. After we got to Tramway Dave had to talk to the fire wardens and some fishermen, so I wandered over to the boardinghouse which was empty at this time of year.

From Tramway we went by rail to Chesuncook Lake. These fifteen miles of rails had been laid through the woods by the Lacroix Company to facilitate the transportation of pulp. Along the way we rode through charming country, much of it a very thick growth of spruce and fir. At one point near a cove on the lakeshore we passed an old abandoned camp on the bank, a place that many years before had given shelter to a lumberman or trapper. At another point atop a knoll we could see a spot where in years gone by there had been a fire, dry black sticks of timber leaning awkwardly in all directions. Far off to the east were the mountains, the top of Mount Katahdin looming above all the others. At the end of the rails was a sort of landing where, we were told, one hundred thousand cord of pulp had been unloaded in one year. At this point we met an old man in a canoe. He had paddled all the way from Chesuncook Village, some thirty miles away, to bring mail to the fire wardens who lived at the Tramway. After chatting with him and taking the mail to pass along, we turned back.

At Tramway we located a pretty little spot near a brook to cook our dinner. I remember a poem which I recited for Dave while I cooked dinner. I had read it many years before.

> There are flowers in the meadow,
> There are clouds in the sky,
> Songs pour from the woodland,
> The water glides by.
>
> Too many, too many,
> For the eye or for ear
> The sights that we see,
> The sounds that we hear.

I had thought of these verses during our ride that day. As we rode it had occurred to me that while Nature is not always tricked out in holiday attire, she is nevertheless always interesting. She may be melancholy and dark today. Tomorrow she will be bright and glittering and scattering perfume. And in a strange way one's own spirit sings in harmony with the day. On drab days we are likely to be somewhat cheerless; on bright ones, full of pep and enthusiasm. Nature even in her aspects which we know so well is full of surprises. The waving of boughs in a storm is new and old to us. We are familiar with sunsets, yet no two are ever alike. The honking of geese flying overhead is a sound we know as well as we know our own voices; still, we look up happily whenever the geese signal their passing. Listening to the lulling sound of small waves washing the shore, we fall into sound sleep and awake refreshed after a delightful cool night.

Next morning I went exploring to try to discover what sort of place Tramway had been in years gone by. I found the huge wire cable which had been brought here with such effort. It lay rusting and half buried under moss and leaves and earth. Consider that this cable had at one time traversed the narrow strip of land about a half-mile between Eagle Lake and Chamberlain Lake. Consider the size of the effort to set the cable in operation. And consider that the cable, engines, and other equipment which must have weighed many tons, were brought here without benefit of roads. It must have been a staggering undertaking. Contemplating it now, years after it was accomplished, one feels awe at its daring and, in a strange way, pride in its success.

Once the logs were put in the water at the end of the tram-way, there arose the problem of floating them to Telos Lake and the east branch of the Penobscot River and thence into Bangor, a distance of more than one hundred and fifty miles. This work was handled by drivers, or river hogs as they were called. Several hundred of them were employed on the job, and their skill and agility in skittering from one floating log to another and in loosening tangled log jams has become proverbial in this part of the world. These men, regardless of their size, were astonishingly fast on their feet and as light and graceful in their movements as ballet dancers. They were expert at handling a peavey or pick pole, a long-handled tool with which they would pry loose timbers which had jammed together in the water. It was on this trip that I learned that when he was quite a young man, Dave had been a river hog. He didn't tell me himself. I overheard two other men talking about him. And I was proud to sense in their talk their opinion that he had been one of the best.

The standard diet of the driving crews in those days of the early 1900s was bread, salt codfish, beanhole beans, and molasses. The cooks on the drives were not equipped as they are today. And they not only had little to cook insofar as variety was concerned, but they also cooked under very difficult circumstances. I suppose a lot of the cooking equipment and provisions were carried along on the floating logs and landed at the river's edge when time came to set up kitchen and prepare a meal. More likely, permanent cook camps were set up along the shore beside the log floats where the river hogs could jump off, get fed, and then continue on their way.

Beanhole beans are so called because of the manner in which they are cooked. First, a hole big enough to hold the pot is dug and thickly lined with glowing wood coals. The tight-covered pot of beans is then placed in the hole, the hole is covered over lightly with earth, and the beans are left to bake for ten or fifteen hours. Some of the old-time cooks kept two beanhole ovens going at one time and thus had a batch of beans cooking at all times. There were huge crews of men to be fed twice a day, and I imagine the cooks were kept good and busy baking bread, preparing salt codfish, and baking beans for one relay after another of hungry men.

Writing of it now I can smell the wonderful aroma of freshly cooked beanhole beans. I think there is no more appetizing odor on earth than that which fills the air when the cover is first removed from a bean pot taken out of a beanhole. Dave and I had a good laugh once when, traveling by car through Maine, we spotted ahead of us a "Beanhole Beans" sign on a little cabin. Dave suggested we stop there for dinner. We did—and it was a nice tidy little place with clean red-and-white-checked

tablecloths. We sat down and ordered, and then while we waited for the beans to be warmed or perhaps to be dug out of the beanhole out back, Dave got up and wandered around the little restaurant. I watched him as he peeked into the kitchen and the change which came over his face was very funny to see. He tiptoes back to our table and whispered, "How would you like some nice
B & M beans fresh from the can for a change?" That's what we had for dinner that night.

While on the lumber drive the men slept in a shed tent with a big fireplace built in front. Around the fire were trousers and stockings to be dried out. However, a good many of these men slept with their wet clothes on. If the ground was level there would be as many as sixty men sleeping on fir boughs under the same tent. The men covered themselves with a heavy quilt or puff blanket which measured thirty-two feet long. These wood quilts would cover from twenty-five to thirty men. If a man got up in the night he would find his place taken when he returned, for someone would have rolled over or stretched in his sleep. Then the man who got up had to seek refuge at the end and hang onto the edge of the quilt. It was not unusual to get up very early in the morning and see ten or fifteen men cuddled up close to the fire. These men had been robbed of their places during the night. This style of blanket was last used in 1922. Today a lumberman and pulp cutter has an individual bed and blanket to lie on.

Dave joined me and we explored many places during the day, looking over sites where the remains of the old camp could be discerned. We followed the old logging road, now merely a deep rut. I find this kind of probing into the past most engrossing. And it fascinates me to the point that I can see the forms of those who used to work and pass over these old logging roads, so many years ago. The same stars and the same moon shine for us, and the deep green of the forest is there for us to see. Truly these waters and this forest are enchanted for those who search the past. But my visit was made especially pleasant because Dave is such a well-informed and interesting guide. He knows the country as well as a fox or a bird. He is perfectly familiar with Nature's handiwork. He is, in short, at home anywhere in the woods. As the years go by I find that the rewards of his companionship in the wilderness are very great.

Eagle Lake was calm this day as we glided over the smooth water from one cove to another. Several fishermen were checked in the usual routine. Bert was not home that evening when we arrived at his camp, and as before we were greeted by all the actresses who beautified his walls. When a camp has been closed for several days there is a kind of dampness that settles inside even during the summer, so Dave made a small fire in the cookstove to get enough heat to dispel it. The fact that the camps are built flat on the ground accounts largely for the dampness. So does the thick roof made up of hand-split shingles, roofing paper, about three inches of packed earth over this, and more hand-split shingles topping it off. However, this thick roof keeps the camp very cool in the summer and stops the heat from escaping in winter.

While my husband went to the spring to get a pail of fresh water I began looking at the pictures on the wall. Although I was not familiar with the movies, I recognized several actresses because I had read about them and seen their photos in magazines and newspapers. I noticed among them Pola Negri; Greta Garbo, who at the time was very young; and Ethel Barrymore, who at that time was even more famous than she is today.

I suddenly realized that Bert must be a most lonely man. This camp so deep in the wilderness was so far from his home that it was seldom his family stayed with him. Now it occurred to me that even though he was very busy with the checking of lumber camps, trappers, fishermen and hunters, and any other men who roam the lumbering country, his life was the lonely kind. Certainly it was more so than the lives of old hermits we encounter here and there in the wilderness, for they have chosen to exile themselves and it is their wish to remain alone.

There is, for example, old Bill Gorden who came here when he was a very young man. He has spent a whole lifetime in a little camp at the head of the St. John River. The trapping he does never amounts to much, some years barely enough to buy food for a year. He never receives any mail except for a fur buyer's list now and then. Now at the age of eighty-five this old hermit is awaiting the end which awaits us all, his lifetime wasted away. Today he is unable to go to the nearest settlement anymore. Some folks are kind enough to take him food and clothing now and then.

Hermits baffle me. I have often wondered what was their aim in life—whether they were driven by disappointment to live in this fashion, or if there was some other urge which the rest of us can't understand, an urge simply to seek solitude for its own sake rather than to flee society out of pique or anger or spite. Frequently, these odd characters are less frugal than you would expect. With so little else to do it would seem reasonable, for instance, for them to cut their firewood a year ahead of time so that it would be dry and ready when wanted. But no, instead of doing such chores, Mr. Hermit will more likely be found, when you call, sitting in front of his camp on the deacon seat, smoking and staring into space. The hermit is not hospitable. He answers you briefly. Dave says of them that they should all crawl into holes and pull the holes in after them.

There are hermits who for reasons of their own escaped the outside world and sought refuge in the big wilderness. Some of these men are very active, however, all alone though they may be. They travel the lumbering country a great deal, sometimes securing a job for a while, only to leave it and go back to their cabins or to do some trapping, hunting, and fishing. They read a lot. They very seldom get any mail. Nevertheless, conversation of any kind seems to be of no interest or importance to them. There are also many who, tired of the hoorah and ballyhoo of city life, seek this big wilderness for its quietness and easy living. These settle down and live contented with all the routine of a woodsman's life. They very seldom work. They seem very happy. The outside world is just the outside world for them, and they want nothing more to do with it.

Another type of hermit we come across now and then also lives alone, in an abandoned camp, but works, usually at farming a small portion of land he has acquired just by simply moving onto it. He keeps animals, a horse, and maybe some cattle, which he will sell to lumber camps during the winter. Once or twice a year he will go to the nearest village and buy food for several months ahead. While there he gets drunk, spends the balance of his money, and then returns home broke. None of them ever marry.

The caretaker, I find, rates in the same class with the hermit, only his work consists in looking after a lumber camp or a dam. His wages usually are very small, but the company provides food for him and he is very saving in general. Often enough he works until he is very old, always for the same company. Then the company arranges for him to be taken into someone's home or perhaps into an old people's home. Some of the companies have very generous and considerate attitudes toward sick old caretakers.

There are also a few couples strongly devoted to one another. The woman follows the man, doing her equal share of the work, hunting and trapping and fishing and hauling. They never marry; they have no children; they simply remain together in the wilderness until they are too old and sick to look after themselves. I know of one such couple who lived like this for twenty-one years with never a sight of the outside world. They were perfectly happy and without a worry.

Another type of very lonely man that I admire very much in this great wilderness is the surveyor. Well educated, highly trained, he is, of course, of an altogether different breed from the hermit. He estimates lumber stands, helps map the country, settles the township lines, and so on. He is capable, intelligent, and healthy. The great outdoors is his home the year round. He sleeps in a tent, carries a heavy pack on his back, travels in all kinds of weather, and very seldom eats a home-cooked meal. These men rarely give up their work until late in life. Although they may have families they seldom get to see them.

My study of these wilderness characters leads me to the conclusion that they age very slowly in comparison to people who live in the city. They are people who are utterly without worries. Even the changing seasons do not concern them particularly. The winter's snow is no more a bother to them than the summer's grass. You could not very well call them woods-queer. They have simply made and stuck to their choice of a way of life.

Chapter 14

Further Adventures

One October we prepared to make a trip to the Allagash. Dave had to attend to some business in that area and he said I could go along if I wished. The morning of the fifth we came to Nine Mile Bridge and put in to the St. John there. We loaded our canoe and left early. Although the water in the St. John River was very low at that time, the current was strong enough to carry us over many of the very shallow places we encountered going through. As we left the shore of the river at Nine Mile I looked back at the bridge which had been such a benefit to so many people whose travels oblige them to cross the St. John River. With the morning sun shining all over it, it made a pretty picture. The leaves were well gone off the hardwood trees and something in the air reminded one strongly that fall was here again. Overhead there was the honking of wild geese on their way south, a sure sign that winter is on the way. Yet it was a mild day, an Indian summer day, one of the last glows of warmth before real cold weather set in.

As we approached the Caron farm at Seven Islands I asked Dave if he would let me get out and walk, for this was the farm I had spent much time at as a child. Many a time I had hunted over it in the fall when my brother and I were young. Now I wanted once more to follow the wagon road along the edge of the river and perhaps get a partridge or two at our favorite old place. Taking my shotgun I went up the bank of the river about a mile from the house. I found myself in what appeared to be a new place. During all the years I had been gone, the little trees I had known had grown enormous and other little fir and spruce trees grew all through the field which years ago had been all cleared, plowed, and planted. After looking for the old wagon-wheel track which was not too difficult to locate, I headed down the road to the house.

I walked slowly while Dave drifted down the river. When I came to a turn in the road I spotted a partridge and lifted my shotgun to my shoulder. I aimed at it once and then again, but finally decided not to shoot. This farm was abandoned now and very few hunters came through here. In a way it was becoming a sort of sanctuary. As the farm became a forest with the passing years, more and more partridges would be about.

When I got to the old house a feeling of sadness came over me. I recalled the many happy days I had spent there with my mother and father and the rest of my family. I remembered the things I used to treasure in my room, little playthings, books, old letters, pieces of wedding cakes and birthday souvenirs kept as tokens. Perhaps some of them might still be there to see. I wondered whether my brother's toys would be there also and my mother's old dishes which she had loved so well. I could see as I approached that there were still a few flowers growing in my mother's flower garden.

As I opened the door I smelled cigarette smoke. Thinking perhaps someone had moved in, I entered the house very slowly. But it was Dave, sitting quietly in the old rocking chair. I was happy to see him there, and together we looked through the tokens I had left. Then we returned to the canoe.

In later years our old home and everything that was in it burned to the ground. I have never returned since.

Leaving Seven Islands behind us we paddled down twelve miles to the Simmons farm. This old farm had long ago been abandoned. Now it was quite heavily overgrown with trees, and two old hermits lived there in the sagging, ramshackle house.

They had a dozen house cats, five dogs, and many boxes of books as one of them did little else but read. By farming and trapping and with the help of a small income from a pension of some sort, they were able to live idly and in as much comfort as they wished. After a bit of conversation with them we continued on to the mouth of the Big Black River just fifteen miles further down the St. John. There we stopped for the night at the fire warden's camp. This man and his wife had been employed by the Forestry Department for a good many years, and remained at the camp the year round.

The mouth of the Big Black River has an interesting historical past. A good many years ago when the Indians occupied this part of the timberland, the Big Black and part of the St. John were in their hunting territory. They farmed some parts of it and raised a great amount of corn. It is said that during an epidemic many of them died and were buried on the point at Big Black. Just a few years ago an expedition came up this way and dug out a number of graves. They found enough relics to prove that the stories about themselves which the Indians had passed on to one another from generation to generation were the truth.

Today, small alders grow all over the cemetery. Yet the burial mounds are still easily visible. I listened one night to an old man from the Allagash Plantation who asserted emphatically that only a few years ago the Big Black was haunted. He claimed that laments and screams were heard in the dead of many a night. Very few people cared to camp there at night. According to the old man the strange night cries stopped all of a sudden and were heard no more. I dare say that a good many people in the vicinity of Allagash believed in ghosts, but to my mind the noises heard at night in the wilderness are accounted for by beings a lot more substantial than ghosts.

After we left Big Black the water was much higher and we soon came to Castongay settlement. This was at one time a large farm, perhaps the largest on the St. John River. Now the place was vacant and only the remains of an old barn could be seen. As we neared the Ouellette farm just a few miles below, we stopped to say hello to the people who lived there. This farm was where Dave had been born and brought up. It was a pleasant spot with a brook running close by the new camp which these people had built. All the buildings were new with the exception of the greenhouse. In later years we often went there and ate our supper right at the mouth of the brook. Fishing is forever good at that place.

When we arrived at the head of the Big Rapids we decided to go through them. The Big Rapids are one mile long. At certain times of the year the going is very good. However, not many people attempt to go through, one way or the other. The rapids are very rocky and ledgy and full of white foamy water all the way down. In the spring when the water is very high, no one in his right mind dares to go through.

We spent a day at my husband's home while he was attending to his business. I welcomed the opportunity to visit with his mother and some other people I had met during the previous visits there, for this was the place where Arlene and Bobby had been born. While this place is situated in the woods it could perhaps be called a village. More properly, I think, it should be called a settlement. There are no stores. People do their shopping from stores on wheels that come up once or twice a week, depending on how much buying is done.

On October the eighth we headed back up to Umsaskis Lake by way of the Allagash River. Because we had to take time to pack and to load the canoe, we did not arrive at Allagash Falls until noon. We found a very nice camping ground there with a fireplace, and we cooked and ate our dinner there while listening to the rumbling of the water falling over a drop of perhaps as high as thirty feet. We continued on up the river after carrying the luggage and canoe around the falls. There are two places to enter the river after leaving the falls. One is very dangerous and only expert canoemen undertake to leave the shore at that point. The upper entry is not too difficult, although the current there is much stronger than at the other place. We used the upper entry.

We once made a trip to the Allagash with the children. On our return trip, after we had left the falls, Arlene was sitting in back of me surrounded by luggage, our lunch box, the sleeping bags, and among other things, a large bag of oranges, precious to us in the woods. While my husband was busy watching where he was going after leaving the first carry, he noticed a few oranges floating past the canoe. Thinking someone had upset he began looking around. Then he noticed that Arlene was dropping them overboard. With much difficulty, as her hands were so tiny, she had already put most of them in the water.

We camped that night at Cunliff Depot. The old camp there was occupied by a solitary caretaker, for the company which had been operating in that territory had long before vacated and given up timber cutting. The caretaker stayed on, making this abandoned camp his home as so many of them do throughout the lumber country.

The next morning we found that the water had dropped, making it impossible to use the outboard motor in some places. So the pole had to be used. At the head of Musquacook Deadwater and Whitiker Brook the canoe had to be hauled over several places. Just two miles below Long Lake Dam, Dave selected a lunch ground in a place no one had ever occupied before. There he made a fireplace, and while I cooked our supper he made a little table out of split logs. We planned to use this place again some time.

After a couple of hours' rest we continued on up to the dam, poling most of the way. Ed Taylor met us at his house and invited us in for a cup of tea and a piece of his gingerbread cake. But if you ever saw him just at the time he took his cake out of the oven, you would be inclined to say no-thank-you when you were offered a piece. He turned the cake over on the table, broke off a corner of it to see how it looked inside, and then laid the corner on top of the rest of the cake. By the time he and his guests were ready for a piece of cake, one of his many cats had jumped up on the table next to the warm cake. Ed always helped himself to the other end of the cake. When a cake of his was half used up he would throw it to the cats and bake a fresh one. He thought nothing of this, but I did. Yet, because it would have been impolite of me to refuse tea and cake, I always ate it without tasting it. This is hard to do but you can learn to do it.

When we arrived at our home camp we found the children had been well taken care of but were very lonesome.

I have mentioned Levi Dow who, as supervisor of the northern district, was my husband's superior. Levi was always very good and considerate to us. He knew that I accompanied Dave on many of his patrols and he raised no objection. Certainly it wasn't standard procedure for wardens' wives to go traipsing over their preserve with them—but we got away with it.

One day Levi phoned and said that on the following day he wanted Dave and the warden from the next district to report to him at Eagle Lake. The next morning as Dave was struggling with his freshly pressed uniform, he said, "Why don't you come along for the ride?"

The idea appealed to me, and a moment later I was hurling myself into my Sunday best while Dave drew on his shiny boots and Sam Browne belt. In no time we were in the car speeding toward Eagle Lake. Levi had summoned Dave and the other warden because a Fish and Game Department seaplane and pilot were available and Levi wanted the two wardens to have a look at their territory from the air. Seaplanes, or those equipped with pontoons, are used in the north of Maine because of the proximity of the many lakes.

When we got to the Dow cottage I settled down to read a book while Levi took Dave and the other man out to the plane, which was anchored at the end of the dock. A few minutes later I was startled to see Levi thrust his head through the window from outside and to hear him boom, "Hey, Annette, how would you like to go along for the ride?"

I jumped up out of my chair as happy as a child. "Do you really mean it?" I said.

"Sure I do," Levi answered. "Hurry up. They're almost ready to go."

I was already slipping on my coat and having a hard job trying not to knock things over in my haste. The idea of flying over the country I loved so well—the idea of getting a bird's-eye view of it—appealed to me so strongly that I could hardly talk because of my excitement.

A moment later I was climbing into the plane, a beautiful four-passenger Stinson on the door of which was a colorful circle bearing the emblem of the Fish and Game Department—a drumming partridge, a jumping trout, and a buck's head. The pilot, a handsome, capable young man, held the door for me while I climbed in and seated myself next to Dave. Then we fastened our safety belts, the pilot got the motor roaring, and we taxied to the end of the lake and turned about. The plane suddenly shook and lurched forward, the water beneath us was churned into a froth, we gathered speed, and the next thing we knew we were airborne.

From the sky the St. John River valley was wonderfully beautiful and, if possible, even more colorful than it appeared to me when I was an earthbound viewer. The erratic courses of streams and brooks which emptied into the St. John, and the St. John itself, took on a character which I had never fully comprehended when I saw them at ground level. The double S of the Allagash River, which pours into the St. John, looked like an enormous green-gray snake. The Allagash Falls, a great tumbling froth of dark blue and white, provided an exciting contrast to the placid quietness of the slow-moving river and the endless stretches of field and forest.

We flew eastward over the Musquacook chain of lakes and the Horse Race which I had heard so much about but had never seen. The Horse Race is a narrow, mile-long strip of very turbulent, foamy white water in the watershed of the Musquacook. As we flew over it Dave told us that many years before he had helped to drive timber logs down the Horse Race and on a couple of occasions had paddled a canoe down it.

We flew over so many of our old haunts that in a way the flight became a brief review of our lives. Churchill Lake, Eagle Lake, Umsaskis. We flew over all of that portion of the Canadian border which bounded my husband's territory. And viewing this vast wilderness from the air made me realize very vividly what an enormous responsibility one man shoulders when he takes over the supervision of such a district. Beneath us the green of the wilderness seemed impenetrable: mile after mile after mile of uninterrupted growth. While it looked barren of any human habitation we knew that concealed within it were some dozens of trappers and hermits. During their seasons hunters and fishermen would swell the population, but even at the height of either season the increase was only a trickle, something that was big only in a relative way.

Here below me, I thought, is the paradise the fishermen and hunters dream so much about: Beau Lake here. Glazier Lake there, the St. Francis River, the Big Black, one after another the favorite spots which sportsmen travel hundreds, sometimes even thousands of miles to get to. And yet, although hunters argued about the particular beauty of their particular favorite spot, from the air there was very little to distinguish one from another.

As we flew over the Big Black, Dave tapped my shoulder and pointed down to the winding river. "Remember the time we took the raft down there with old Uncle Din?" he said.

It came back to me very clearly and I smiled as I recalled the details. Uncle Din had been one of our best-skilled guides and trappers. By some sort of special arrangement with one of the lumber companies in the district, he had permission to gather and keep for his own use cedar poles which had not passed inspection—any amount he wished. Uncle Din was a hardworking man and a methodical and ingenious one. He worked out a system of gathering great quantities of these poles, binding them together into one big raft on the river, and floating them down to a sawmill where he had them cut up into shingles which he then sold at a very tidy profit.

Dave had nudged me to recall the time when he and I had helped Uncle Din wire-lash his raft together and then had accompanied him on it down the Big Black and St. John rivers to Allagash. Our canoe was perched high and dry in the middle of the huge raft of cedar poles which measured seventy-five feet long by thirty feet wide. You can imagine how many shingles the mill later turned out.

I settled back comfortably on the raft on my canoe chair and enjoyed every minute of the long ride. Dave and Uncle Din manned huge poles, which they used to steer the raft, and their cries to one another to watch out for this or that obstruction, to push this way or that, were very pleasant to hear in the otherwise soundless wilderness.

Uncle Din had an old washtub aboard in which he kept spike nails to be used in case the raft showed signs of breaking up. And when Dave and he, after several hours, began to talk about how hungry they were and where would be a good place to head the raft in to shore for dinner, I prevailed upon them to keep the raft moving downriver and to let me build a fire in the washtub and cook our meal over it. We had some beefsteak and potatoes and canned goods with us, and I whipped up a meal which really must have been good, for Dave and Uncle Din tore into it like a pair of wolves.

Later on in the afternoon we had neared Big Rapid, and since the raft was holding together very nicely Dave had let me stay aboard. There had been some talk of making me go ashore and walk from the start to the end of the rapids. The huge bulk of the raft made the ride down the rapids less exciting than I had expected it to be, but it was fun nevertheless. We got through without incident and late that afternoon arrived at Allagash after having covered forty miles during the day.

The banking of the plane put an end to these reveries and I suddenly realized that we were about to land at Dow's Point. We

circled and landed smoothly. Levi was there on the wharf looking at his watch.

"You were gone a little over two hours," he said as we
climbed out. "How was it?"

Dave and the other warden and I all started to gabble at
once and I, especially, to thank Levi. I found it difficult to tell
him how grateful I was—but I know that he sensed how I felt,
for he patted me on the shoulder and said, "I'm glad you were
able to go."

I spent many days hunting along the private road that ran
near our camp at Umsaskis Lake, often taking along the children
and Jeanne, the girl who was keeping house for me. On one of
the expeditions we ran into some quite unpleasant trouble. At
about three in the afternoon one day, two men from the Allagash
Plantation, who knew my husband well, knocked at my door and
asked if I could possibly drive them up to Churchill Lake. I forget what it was that made their request so urgent, but it seemed
important at the time, and I said sure, I would drive them.

Jeanne and the children came with me. The trip up was nice,
but I sensed that the car was not running as smoothly as usual.
So when I arrived at Churchill I left the boys at the office and
continued to the company garage. I told the man my trouble and
asked him if he could repair whatever it was. He added water
to the battery, as the lights on the car were very low, and he did
something to the fuel pump. Then he told me everything was
all right and we started back. It was dusk when we left Churchill
and the car seemed to be going along nicely. But about five miles
from our camp it backfired, sputtered a few times, and then

stopped. Jeanne and I pushed the car off the road and climbed in to wait for the first one who came along.

There were very few cars on the road at this time of day and I was seriously concerned over how long we would have to wait. Darkness, deep black darkness, came very early. Fortunately Dave always keeps a couple of woolen blankets in the car, along with an ax, a shovel, and a flashlight. We bundled the children in the two blankets and held them close. Jeanne was in tears when she asked what we would do if we had to spend the night there. After what seemed to be three hours we saw the lights of an approaching car. The driver stopped to talk with us for a few minutes and find out what the trouble was. I explained that we had broken down and asked whether he could give us a lift into the camp. I pointed out that we had three children with us and that they were shivering with cold.

The driver spoke to his wife for a second and then replied, "We're sorry, but we just can't. We just received a telegram that one of our relatives died and we must hurry along for the funeral in the morning."

They drove off and that was that. I dare say that the word I said in farewell wasn't nice at all. Jeanne again began to cry. I tried to talk sense to her but it was no use. The children were by now asleep and, wrapped as they were in the blankets, warm. Jeanne nevertheless insisted they would freeze. I said before that happened I would take the ax and cut some dry wood and make a fire beside the car. With the door open to the fire we would all be warm.

After an hour or two more we spotted a light coming over the big hill at Umsaskis. In no time the vehicle, a large truck loaded with hay and oats, stopped and the driver hopped out to ask what was the trouble. For a second time we repeated our story. He asked if we could hold out a while longer while he took his load to Churchill and then came back to take us home. He told us how long it would take and then departed.

At eleven o'clock that night he returned. As we came onto the road going into our camp he shook his head, saying the road was not safe for a large truck and that he was afraid he'd get stuck in the mud if he continued. So Jeanne and I set out for the camp afoot. I led Arlene by the hand and Jeanne followed with Hilda in her arms and Bobby stumbling along sleepily beside her. We finally had to carry Bobby and Arlene too, for they could not walk as fast as we wished to. Soon enough our camp showed up in the beam of our flashlight and we were home at last. Jeanne said, "I'm not going anywhere for a long time." I didn't tell her I had almost been in tears myself while we were on the road.

When Dave called from Churchill two days later to ask me to come and pick him up in the car, I told him what had happened to us and explained that the car was still broken down alongside the road. Furthermore, since we had left it, a seventeen-inch snow had fallen. But it was Dave's problem from this point on, and before long he and some of his friends retrieved the car and got it in working order again.

Chapter 15

Eight-Point Buck

I made one trip into the Little Pleasant Lake area which lies to the east of Churchill Lake at the head of a small stream emptying into the latter. Dave was going on an inspection tour through some of the lumber camps there and he said that I would probably be able to get my deer in that vicinity. So I packed for the trip, dressed up in warm clothes, and gave my .32 Winchester Special a careful going over. We headed for Churchill Lake very early one morning two weeks before the close of the hunting season.

Bright and early we arrived at Churchill and soon found ourselves on the tote road to Big Pleasant Lake. Now in mid-November there were two feet of snow on the ground. The ridges were all white and tracks could be seen far in the distance. The road was smooth, and traveling on foot was easy. The first camp we would come to lay thirteen miles ahead. Chipmunks and red squirrels chattered noisily as we made our appearance around each bend in the road, jumping excitedly ahead of us from branch to branch. Little winter birds flew in waves from patches of hay and oats that had fallen from the toters' sleds. As soon as we passed they fluttered back and continued their pecking. We could see one of the toters' sleds far up the road ahead of us and it appeared that we were gaining on it.

At the edge of Big Pleasant Lake, which was halfway to the first lumber camp, we stopped to lunch. But before eating we walked to the shore to look over the lake. At once my husband spotted a deer being chased across the ice by a large dog followed by a smaller one. All of a sudden the deer went through the ice not far from the shore. Both dogs stood at the edge of the hole, barking.

Starting on the run Dave shouted at me not to come as the lake was clear ice and very slippery. We now discovered that the tote-sled driver had also stopped at the lakeshore, and Dave yelled to him, asking him to give me a lift into the camp. I replied that I wanted to go with him. But he didn't listen and rushed on toward the deer in the hope of saving it. I thought I would follow anyway. But I had gone less than a hundred yards when my feet slipped from under me and down I went, hitting my head a solid crash on the ice. My .32 Special flew into the air and hit the ice twenty feet from where I lay. It slid about twenty feet farther when it hit the ice. I saw stars all over the lake. When my head cleared I looked across the lake to see Dave too far away now to follow.

Dave had certainly been right. The ice was too slippery for me. I finally got to my feet just as the toter reached me. He thought I had been seriously hurt. I returned to the lunch place listening to the toter tell me I had been lucky not to fracture my skull. He offered me a cup of tea and insisted I eat with him. Dave could no longer be seen on the lake. The deer had managed to scramble out of the water and to dash into the woods on the other side of the lake. Dave, I knew, was now more interested in doing away with the two dogs. When the sled team was all through feeding I got on the load and rode the remaining miles to the first camp. I knew my husband would get there sometime during the afternoon.

I waited by the stove in the cook room chatting with the cook and sipping cup after cup of hot tea. After a couple of hours Dave came in, looked at me for a few seconds, and then smiled, saying, "How's your head? Will you mind me next time I tell you the ice is slippery?" The cooks looked at each other, wondering what was what. So Dave told them what had happened and even I had to join in the laughter. Dave reported that the deer had gotten safely away and that he had managed to kill the dogs with just two shots. When I combed my hair the next morning, I had good reason to remember the slick ice of Big Pleasant.

After resting awhile we set out again, as we had three more miles to go to the camp at Little Pleasant where we would stay during our time in that territory. The afternoon sun was sinking from view behind the mountain at our right as we arrived at our destination. It was the first time I had visited Little Pleasant and I enjoyed it immensely. Although my legs were getting a little lame I knew that after a few hours' rest I would be fit again.

To some people, traveling through the woods may seem monotonous. I, for one, have always found it exciting. I am one of those whom every prospect pleases. For me and for Dave the woods are always new and full of surprises. The surprise may be as simple a thing as a tree grown out of shape and forming a picture of something. Or it may be a giant pine tree—we have frequently stopped to examine such trees closely and to try to guess how many feet of lumber there was in them. Or it may be a very old stump cut half a century ago.

I have for many years been in the habit of getting myself a chew of spruce gum the minute I enter the forest. Frequently this involves getting off the trail in search of a spruce tree. And I think I enjoy the search for the right tree as much as I do the gum itself. I recall doing just this one time when Dave came back to see what I was up to. He found me digging at an old spruce tree for a chew of gum. He said, "That gum is no good. See the mark of a bear's claw on the bark? And the bear's hair all over the gum?" I was more choosy from then on.

The camp we were to stay at was built on a small island in the middle of the lake. Dave sounded the ice with his ax and called to me to follow him. I remembered my fall earlier in the day and my head began aching all over again. The island on which the camp was built was about fifteen hundred feet long and three hundred feet wide. Fir, spruce, white birch, cherry trees, and one large pine grew on it. A few trees had fallen—either from age or the beatings of severe storms.

A little cabin had been built at the lower end of the island about ten feet from the water's edge. The bank was very low and a path beaten down by a few fishermen led from the cabin door. The cabin, fourteen by twenty feet, was built of small identical logs peeled and dried in the sun. They were positively golden in color. The roof was made of hand-split cedar shingles all of an even size. The camp inside was furnished with cupboards, a table, two benches, and a tin stove with an oven. There was a single bed. All in all, it was a tidy, comfortable, warmly habitable little camp. I fell in love with it the minute I set eyes on it. Looking at it from the shore when the sun was shining its rays all over it, I had the feeling that it was enchanted. As far as I was concerned it was the most beautiful cabin in the world.

We cooked our supper and baked a small pan of biscuits. Tom had finally decided to show me how to mix biscuit batter. I asked him if he would bake the biscuits for supper. "Gladly," he had said. "And I'll show you so you can begin to do your own baking."

Standing by his side I was all attention. When he was ready to put in the rising soda and cream of tartar he said, "Don't be afraid to put in a lot." He emptied two rounded teaspoonfuls into the batch as he said this, then added a wee bit more. "Then," he went on, "you add your melted fat, then water. Just enough. And roll, cut, and bake."

But poor Tom! When his batch was baked it was not what he had planned to have. He had used far too much soda, and his biscuits were hardly fit to eat. Tom was very cross. He said, "I think if you keep on doing them your way, they'll be all right."

We started our trip again early in the morning after a good night's rest and a breakfast of bacon, jelly, and bread toasted over the coals. We took along a lunch which I had packed. Making our way into the road which was used for hauling timber, we followed it to the landing. There my husband spoke to several men who were employed on the haul. Then we continued down the north side of the lake. We could now see the tracks of deer, bobcats, and foxes. Game was plentiful in that part of the forest and I was all eyes in my search for the buck deer I wanted so badly. After walking slowly for twenty minutes looking from one side of the road to the other, we came face to face with a large deer. He stood like a statue looking at me and I stopped in my tracks, my heart beating much too fast, my hands clutching the rifle so hard they hurt.

My husband whispered to me to get my rifle ready. I couldn't take my eyes off the deer. I told Dave to get him, but he refused. Then I raised my rifle, aimed at the buck once, and then lowered the rifle. I looked at Dave, then at the deer. And then, for the second time, I lifted my rifle to my shoulder. This time I pulled the trigger. At the first shot the deer dropped to the snow. I could not believe that I had hit him until I approached and examined him. In my nervousness in aiming at his shoulder, I had shot him an inch below the right eye. I deposited a kiss on my old .32 Special and put my arms around Dave's neck to give him a good hug.

Getting a dead deer back to camp is quite an experience, since it takes a lot of strength and more resourcefulness than you would guess. I did everything I could to help, but getting the animal over fallen logs and under and around matted bushes and out to the lakeshore was very tiring. Once we were on the iced-over lake the going was fairly easy. The buck weighed a hundred and seventy-five pounds. He had a beautiful set of antlers counting eight points.

This had been quite a day after the unpleasant experience of the day before, but the excitement of shooting my buck gave me a splitting headache. We decided to remain in the cabin the rest of the day. Our conversation was all buck deer, the way it had looked at us and so forth. I soon began to worry over the way I had shot the deer and to tell my husband of the many people I had heard say that if a deer was shot in the face it was shot by the glare of a jack light. I said this would look bad for me when people got a look at my prize. Dave laughed and told me to forget about it.

It was late when we sat down to a supper of fried deer liver and onions, hot biscuits, and applesauce. Speaking of liver, we had several times eaten porcupine liver which tasted very good. Levi Dow once made a trip to Ross Lake with my husband and on their return they brought with them the livers of three porcupines which Levi prepared and fried himself. They tasted much like pork liver, but much more tender, and were prepared as you would prepare any kind of liver.

Simply because other meats are not often available, woodsmen get to know and like wild meats. Beaver tail can be cooked very tasty. The tail is split and when the skin is removed, a firm meat resembling fish is left. The tail is then cut up and parboiled in water with salt and a bit of soda. This done, the water is drained off and the beaver tail fried in hot salt-pork fat. It is very tender and tastes fishy—but good. Some of the trappers roast beaver meat like beef or pork. Beaver meat is the same color as beef.

Bear meat is another of the trapper's delicacies. Many sportsmen relish bear meat and it is sold in the big cities at high prices. Fried or roasted the meat is very appetizing and smells, as it cooks, like western beef. It is very dark and tender but also very fat. In their day the Indians broiled it over the open fire. Muskrat and raccoon are also eaten in the woods. Like the bear they are fatty enough to provide the makings for soap.

Our supper was delicious, but my appetite had vanished because of all the excitement of the day. Nevertheless, Dave begged me to eat, as the next day was to be a long and busy one. Early the next morning we walked over to the lumber camp at the foot of Little Pleasant Lake, and while Dave inspected the camp for guns and traps, I went into the cook room for a bit of conversation with the cook. I told him of my deer and he was glad to hear about it. Then he began telling me some recipes and even wrote some of them down for me so that I would be sure to remember them. One I'll never forget is for "strawberry" jam. It is made up with three cups of white sugar, one can of tomatoes, and two cups of water. These are boiled together until thick. This makes one quart of "strawberry" jam, woodsman-style. It is wonderful on pies. It sounds almost unbelievable but you will find it is worth the try. Some of the lumberman cooks manage to produce a remarkable variety of desserts merely by mixing flour, sugar, lard, and water or milk. When an assortment of bottles of flavor extracts is available, they perform real wonders.

We continued on to the cuttings and by noon came upon a crew of men eating their dinner. They begged us to join them, for they had plenty of food and a big pot of tea. We took out our own lunch but helped ourselves to some warm beans and hot tea. Then we headed for the Clear Lake area. We got to this lake, which is the headwater of the Musquacook chain of lakes, by following roads through the cuttings of logs and pulp. The country we covered was pretty much cleared of timber. Only the hardwood remained untouched, and what few fir and spruce there were were too small to cut down. Clear Lake at this time of year was frozen all over and the ice was mirror-like with the patches of bright blue and white in the sun. It is a large lake and very appropriately named. Even experienced guides and fishermen say that its water is very deceiving. You may paddle over what you think is very shallow water only to find that its depth is well beyond the reach of the tip of your paddle.

As we stood on the high bank looking over the entire lake and the surrounding mountains, my husband began telling me of the time when he first became a warden. On his first trip here he had stayed with Bert Morrison, who was fire warden in charge of the tower. On this particular rainy day Bert did not go to the tower but worked around the camp. In the afternoon he and Dave had spotted a bear swimming not far away. In Bert's sixteen-foot canoe they took after the bear. With both paddling, it did not take long to overtake him. But as they neared the bear it turned around with its ugly mouth wide open and began to swim toward the canoe. Dave and Bert were unarmed so they did a quick turn-about and paddled for the shore as fast as they could go. They made the landing all right. Mr. Bear made his getaway up a thirty-five-foot-high bank after slipping and falling back into the water just above the camp. It didn't take Dave long to learn that such foolhardy adventures more often than not end in tragedy.

Afterward we went on to a group of sporting camps. These were closed at this time of the year but it was easy to see what a perfect setup they were for a fisherman. The fishing is excellent in Clear Lake, and a great many fishermen spend their vacations there. These camps were precisely what the brochures call them—a fisherman's paradise.

I have often tried to decide which of the lakes in this area is the most beautiful. Chamberlain Lake with its wide expanse of water, or Eagle Lake with its beautiful island; Churchill Lake for the beauty of its water just before a storm, or perhaps Cliff

Lake with the colorful ledges which encircle it. Or perhaps it is
Harrow Lake or Spider Lake or Big Pleasant or Little Pleasant,
which live up to their names so well. Clear Lake or Umsaskis . . .
How could anyone ever make up his mind and come to a defi-
nite, final choice? They are all so beautiful.

It was after dark when we returned to the little cabin. I fried
another mess of deer liver and onions for our supper. Some people fry any kind of liver until it is tough as a shoe sole. A cook in
a lumber camp once told me how to prepare liver properly. He
told me never to use any fat other than salt pork. Slice the liver
thin, then roll it in flour. Fry it quickly on both sides, turning it
several times until it is nicely brown. It always turns out tender
when cooked in this fashion. I have also had good luck with
roast liver, preparing it in much the same way as one prepares
roast beef. With a little thickening added to it, the juice makes
wonderful gravy.

After five days we headed for home. My buck deer was
brought out to Churchill on the toter's team while we traveled
on foot. We arrived at Churchill Lake late in the afternoon. The
team was already there and several men were admiring the deer.
They congratulated me on my good fortune and on my good
shot. These men happened to be French and the toter was telling
them about it in the French language.

"*La femme du garde-chasse Jackson a tué un chevreuil.*"

They replied, "*À quelle place?*"

The toter replied, "*Au Petit Plaisir Lake.*"

Then one of the men said, "*Nom-de-nom, comme elle est
chanceuse, la petite femme.*"

It was like old times listening to this French conversation.
After loading our belongings in our car and lashing the deer onto
a front fender, we set out for our home camp, happy over the
wonderful hunting trip we had had.

Tom Sweeney was no more now—I feel very sad even at the mention of his name. It all happened this way. Three weeks before the Fourth of July he began to complain that he had a pain in his chest. Dave suggested that he go to the doctor but Tom, an old woodsman, insisted that a little drink of soda would do him just as much good.

During the early part of the summer he had asked me to go fishing, as he frequently did. Thinking nothing of it, I went along. On our way back from fishing I was bragging about our nice catch of trout when, looking up, I noticed that he was not sitting in his usual place on the seat in the stern of the canoe, but flat in the bottom of the boat and paddling in that awkward position. I did not speak of it or ask him why he sat that way, but I looked at him closely. I could see a great change in him that I had never noticed before. His face looked drawn and yellowish and he looked very thin and tired. Without showing my fright, I reached for my paddle and began to help him. The quicker we got home the better.

I realized all at once that Tom was a very sick old man and that his wish was to die at Umsaskis Lake and nowhere else. I told my husband of my feeling and commented that I was now afraid to have Tom come to stay with us lest he pass away in the middle of the night. At the same time we did not want to hurt the poor soul. He had always been as kind and thoughtful as a father to us.

But God took care of everything, for on the morning of the Fourth of July, going fishing to his favorite place with one of the boys he knew so well, Tom suffered a heart attack and fell overboard. Had he been all alone he would never have been found, but the young man hauled him into the canoe and brought him back to the camp. God had granted Tom his greatest wish. We did miss him for a long while and we often talk about him even now. Tom is unforgettable.

Chapter 16

Dave is Transferred

A game warden's work year after year is pretty much the same. There are a number of arrests each year. In some cases the same man is arrested many times. Fall patrolling grew more and more rigid as the years went by; most of it had to be done on the lakes that hunters could reach by car. I still accompanied my husband on many of these night patrols. Often I would stand watch while he checked places a little farther off. I had learned by then to identify the noises a human being makes, such as the swish of a paddle in the water, footsteps sounding along the shore, and so on.

November is a busy time for the wardens. The geese and ducks have undertaken their great migrations south and we no longer see the living clouds of them which earlier settled on our lakes and ponds. But now is the time when everyone thinks of the buck he would like to shoot, the big one that got away last year and must be so much bigger this year. In my own case I was thinking with excitement of the big buck I had seen all through summer season. Many a time I had seen him, sometimes traveling back and forth on the main road. By fall he had a huge set of horns. We could count at the least twelve points. His chest was wide, and by the looks of him he would weigh much over two hundred pounds.

It was a lively guessing game all through the hunting season—I soon found out I was not the only one watching for him. I saw him at least ten times. One glimpse of him was all you could get. With a jump and a wave of his white flag he would bound to a more secure spot.

On November the second our first snowstorm made its appearance and we knew then that the snow was here to stay. My husband made a trip to Churchill Lake and Eagle Lake. There he met Game Warden Grant, who had replaced Bert Duty. Bert, who had been in that country for a good many years, was retiring from the service. Warden Grant came from Bangor, where he had been a city cop for several years. He was a big jolly fellow and very friendly. My husband introduced him to that part of the wilderness and their first trip together was to the Musquacook area.

In mid-December Dave caught a man red-handed breaking one of the game laws. I forget just what law the man was breaking and just how Dave caught him. In any case, after apprehending this fellow, Dave had to take him to the nearest judge—a journey involving sixty-five miles cross-country on snowshoes over unbeaten trails and thereafter thirty miles behind a team of hired horses. This must have been a horrible lesson for the culprit because he was a man who was clumsy on snowshoes and the snow was deep and difficult. They stopped at Priestly Rapids to eat and then continued on to Simmons' farm where they spent the night. That first day they covered twenty-four miles. They got as far as Morel Shed the following night. On the third day they hired a team at the Ouellette farm and got to Fort Kent after dark. On the fourth day the judge at Fort Kent levied a stiff fine against the lawbreaker. I have always had a strong feeling that the culprit was a lot more impressed by his forced march with Dave than he was by the fine, and I suspect that thereafter he paid respectful attention to the state's game laws.

People get into the habit of accepting the services of their law-enforcement officers as just something that's all in the day's work. In a sense that is, of course, so. Like anyone else, in taking on their jobs, game wardens oblige themselves to do well. Occasionally, however, there are exceptional circumstances. This seemed to me to be a striking example—the sort of extra effort soldiers and policemen and firemen are called on to make now and then, but civilian workers almost never.

While at Fort Kent Dave learned that all the wardens had to attend school for two weeks at Orono to familiarize themselves with a series of new rules which were about to be put into effect. He wired me as soon as he got his orders and advised me to go to my father's house at Lac Frontiere and stay there until the course ended. In a particular way this was unfortunate, for Christmas was just around the corner and it meant that Dave would be separated from the children and me. However, there was no choice—so on the twentieth of December I phoned Charlie Hafford, the mailman, and asked him if he could drive the children and me from Umsaskis to Lac Frontiere.

Charlie agreed to meet me the next morning at the point where the road to our camp left the main road. The next morning I packed our light new sled with the things we would need during our visit with my father, hitched up our dog team, and bundling the children onto the sled, set out for the highway. It was a clear, sunny day, but the thermometer registered ten below zero as we left our camp. There was Charlie at the end of the road waiting for us, a trailer sled hitched onto the back of his car. We loaded the dogs, the sled, and most of our duffel into the trailer sled and then piled into Charlie's car and headed for Lac Frontiere.

The Christmas holiday at my father's house was very pleasant—except for the fact that Dave was not there to enjoy it with us. This was the first time we had been separated at this season, and although there were many people around I was lonesome for Dave. At least I had the consolation of not being alone at Umsaskis.

Arlene went to her first Midnight Mass with my father that Christmas and I couldn't quite get over it. She looked so little and seemed so pleased to be taken along. I have never quite forgotten the sight of her going off hand in hand with my father in the starlight.

On January eighth Dave came back from the course to meet us at Umsaskis. Once again we phoned Charlie, this time to ask him to pick us up and bring us back to our camp. When he dropped us at the main road there wasn't a sign of a trail into our camp. We found it almost completely buried under snow.

That winter was a particularly enjoyable one: We had the dog team, and the children were older and easier to care for. Several times we went down to Clayton on the old California Road to visit Dot Burnham, the postmistress. We would return cold and ravenously hungry just in time for a good hot supper. Twelve miles of dogsledding certainly gives one a good appetite. The main road was beaten down smooth, and if we met a car or truck we clambered up the ten-foot-high snowbank and hung onto the sled and waited until the road was clear again.

Our favorite trail could be seen from our front window. It took us up onto the ridge, then down among thick fir and spruce trees. There we could almost always see several snowshoe rabbits crossing the trail ahead of us, and now and then a partridge. We loved the sharp turn in the trail. The dogs would make a run for it. The fine snow kicked up by the dogs made our faces tingle. Behind us we left a little spray of snow powder tossed up by the sled runners.

In February of 1938 we received word of the death of Roland Conners, chief of the Allagash district. A week later the district was offered to my husband. He accepted, mainly because the children were nearing school age and the transfer would move us into a situation where access to a school would be much easier.

It was with an ache in my heart that I began packing for our move. I hated to bid good-bye to that part of the timberland and to all those beautiful lakes. Now that I looked back on them, my years in that part of the wilderness were all too short. They were time enchanted, just as all the forests and lakes thereabouts were enchanted places.

We had to leave many of our things at the camp. Every item we packed away was a reminder of the happy years gone by—our bookshelves, the little cupboard with the glass doors in which we kept our dishes, the table with the varnished top, the gay carpet which matched the golden color of the spruce logs on the cabin wall. We also had to leave the painted box nailed onto the wall way up over the desk where we had always kept our ammunition.

Our packing lasted only a few days. On the last day Warden Wilson and his wife came up from Nine Mile Bridge and we had a farewell party. The next day our belongings, which had to be sent by express, were taken to Lac Frontiere. The children and I left for Churchill Lake to stay at the home of new warden Grant and his wife. From the Grants, we would take a plane to Allagash Plantation.

One of the foremen who had come to spend the evening at the Grants' told us that the company would not be operating for more than a year or two more as the timber was pretty well cut down. I was strangely pleased at the thought of this happening, for that meant to me that this wilderness would once again become silent except for the song of the birds, the thumping of rabbits' feet, and the drumming of partridges. In the years ahead this great timberland would again be virgin forest.

The next afternoon we bade the Grants good-bye and boarded the plane for the trip down to our new house at Allagash

Plantation. As we left Churchill Lake I looked down over the places we had known so well and had been to so many times. I recognized the brooks we had fished in and I suddenly understood why Spider Lake was so called. Chase Carry on the Allagash, which was frozen at this time of the year, reminded me of a white ribbon stretched out over a dark carpet. The Musquacook Lakes over to the eastward of the Allagash River, that my husband had visited so many times on his patrols, were now only a white blanket of snow in the evergreen forest. How beautiful it all was from the air!

When we flew over Umsaskis Lake I was unable to give our home camp a last look, for my eyes were filled with tears. Then all of a sudden I felt a jerk. The plane dropped forward and then as quickly rose again. I quickly looked at the pilot. He was smiling and shouted to me, "Keep your chin up. Everything will be okay in your new home." How I wished he was right. As I had done on my first trip to the wilderness, I was wondering what our life would be like in this new place.

Forty-five minutes later we landed in the middle of the St. John River, about half a mile from the house I was to live in. With our three children, a suitcase, and a bundle of blankets, I stood on the shore for a few minutes not knowing which way to go. I looked up over the high, snow-rimmed banks of the river that I would have to climb. Suddenly I noticed two boys on top of the bank. Out of curiosity they had come to see why the plane had landed. I waved to them, making signs for them to come to my rescue. With much hardship we climbed the steep, slippery bank of the river, carrying the children who were then beginning to feel the cold of an early spring day. We hiked across three hundred yards of open field to the main highway and thence down a quarter of a mile of paved road to our new home.

Dave had built this house several years earlier for his mother, sisters, and brothers, and all of them were still living in it when we arrived. While it was big and furnished well enough, it was in pretty sad need of paint and wallpaper. Dave's mother, who had recently suffered a paralyzing stroke, was sitting in her wheelchair when we arrived. One of his sisters was scrubbing the kitchen floor. The rest of the family were away for the day—and when they returned in the evening, I had the uncomfortable feeling that our descent upon them wasn't an unmixed blessing. Our arrival meant that some of my in-laws were going to have to move over. The house would now be crowded.

I was given the front bedroom which overlooked the banks of the Allagash River about four hundred feet away. The prospect from this room was very attractive: clusters of fir and spruce, open fields, a knoll, a portion of the river, and up in the other direction, a good unobstructed view of one of the Allagash rapids. In years to come I learned to read the colors of these rapids so accurately that I could almost without error foretell the weather after a brief study of them. Later on when our son Robert was only eight he learned to maneuver his canoe and outboard down these rapids in a way which made Dave as proud as a peacock and me as frightened as a hen.

Chapter 17

The Allagash Plantation

Although Allagash Plantation is the largest in Maine, its population is just a little over a hundred families. Despite this slight population, the scattered community is serviced by two churches and five elementary schools. This had always been my husband's hometown and all of his relatives resided here. I recall that during the first week after we moved here he said one morning, "Annette, don't ever say anything about anybody, for in doing so you will be talking about everyone. They are that closely related."

I could not say that I loved this settlement. A good many of the people seemed strange to me after my years of isolation. And the interrelationship throughout the village was so close and so intertwined that an outsider—which I was—would have to be Dale Carnegie himself to get along without misunderstandings.

I used to call my husband the unwanted man, for very few liked to be seen with a game warden. I learned later on that anyone going to visit a game warden's house stood a good chance of being accused of reporting on someone else.

Many small-town people cannot be made to realize that the game warden is a friend of the public. Somehow they don't stop to consider that in keeping the game intact and in hunting down poachers and other lawbreakers, he is saving the game for all, for this generation and for others to come.

We became used to having only a few friends.

However, in the years we have spent in Allagash Plantation many of our old friends from Umsaskis have come to pay us visits.

These and some newly made friends at the Plantation have made our life a happy one.

When we moved to the new territory my husband assured me that I would in time love this part of the wilderness. But it took me several months to get settled and to feel at home. Even though we were all together, for a long time I felt quite blue and lonesome.

During my first summer at the Plantation I slowly adapted to the life on the farm. I found myself learning to milk the cows and taking care of the chickens and sheep. I was soon left alone to care for Dave's mother, a nine-room house, and our three children. Not used to so much to do, I became very tired and run-down. After several months of this existence we hired a girl to help with the work. Bertha was a reliable girl, a good house-keeper, and a good cook. After a while my husband repaired a small house he owned near the big one and moved his mother into it permanently. His sister Lucy went along to look after her. This arrangement was more congenial all around since it enabled both families to go on living in the manner to which they were accustomed without either imposing on or being beholden to one another.

As the summer went by, the fields and the woods turned bright and pleasant in the sunshine and I began to feel a friend-lier disposition toward my new home. At sunset many evenings I stood on the hill opposite our house and looked down at the long stretch of the St. John River. It struck me then that I had never before realized what a lovely river it was. And now, the longer I am acquainted with it, the more I appreciate it.

From this site near my home, the St. John is visible for almost two miles. It sweeps in a semicircle around the hills and is the central line of a broad valley. Nearer the base of the hills one sees the shadows of every tree and rock. The rich colors of sunsets here are reflected on the peaceful bosom of the river, and I find them breathtaking. The St. Francis River, which flows into the St. John to the northeast of Allagash, is a narrow strip of water, dead in some parts and fast in others. Several brooks empty into it, making fishing ideal. The banks of the river are high all the way, and the water stays very low through the summer months.

When I first moved to the Plantation I felt that it would be proper for me to make some friendly overtures to some of the old folks in the community. So one day I visited one old lady who lived only a short way from my home. She was very nice, welcomed me, and I continued to visit her off and on.

On one of those visits I invited her and her husband to have dinner with us on a Sunday. She refused, saying, "You know, I was born across the river three miles from here. My sisters and brothers still live there, but I have never gone to visit them for thirty-two years. Besides, I haven't been on the hill near your home for twenty-four years."

I was stupefied. Here was a couple who for some reason which I could never understand chose to isolate themselves almost as thoroughly as some of the hermits and recluses I had known back in the Umsaskis area. Here they were, village dwellers, yet they had never set foot in the church or the store or, I suppose, in the houses of any of their neighbors. They were content to limit their activities within their own four walls and along the path to their own spring. And apparently the life agreed with them. The old man didn't die until he was ninety-nine years old. Oddly enough, the couple reared a large family and the children have married and settled near the old folks and fallen into a very similar way of life.

During evening visits with some of the old-timers hereabouts, I have listened raptly to their conversation, for these old
people are full of fascinating and valuable stories about the old
days. Once in a while one of them could be persuaded to sing
one of the old songs made up by some anonymous lumberman
years ago. These songs, sung endlessly around the lumbermen's
campfires on nights years and years ago, have lived on here in the
memory of later generations. They are rather awkward ballads of
purely local interest, songs which record the deeds and fights and
loves of individuals who lived in these parts before most of us
were born. They tell of hardships, camp life, the routine happenings of long-forgotten days.

Dave's new district began at the Big Black Rapid on the
upper St. John River and continued on down to where the St.
Francis River flows in. Then turning up the St. Francis it followed
the Canadian boundary all the way up to Beau Lake, through
a succession of small ponds and Glazier's Lake, all of which are
divided from each other by thoroughfares. This country is more
mountainous than the area around Umsaskis Lake, but it is not
so wild, as the Canadian side of the boundary is inhabited and
is mostly farming country. The Big Black River, the Little Black
River, and the St. Francis all rise in Canada and empty into the
St. John, or, as many woodsmen call it, the Maine River. Thus
Dave's new territory took in the watersheds of these three streams
which lie in the most northerly part of the state of Maine.

My husband's work in this territory was pretty much the
same as it had been at Umsaskis. Instead of the many lakes he
had previously had to patrol, he now had rivers. All in all, he
liked the new district and knew the country well. I soon learned

to love the rivers and the few lakes we had around us. Little Black River became my favorite of all. Yet often during nights when I could not sleep, my thoughts returned to Umsaskis and the wonderful life I had had there.

Dave's patrolling included many miles along the Canadian boundary, beginning at St. Francis and extending to the East Lake area. As before, he traveled alone. During the winter he moved about most of the time on snowshoes. During the summer months his chief means of scouting a good part of the boundary which divides Maine and Canada was his canoe.

The number of men in the woods was not nearly as great as it had been in the Umsaskis district. Nevertheless, many poachers roam the timberland and game was so scarce that in his travels Dave seldom saw a deer—never a moose—and only a few bears. Several companies had for a number of years been operating in this section during the summer, fall, and winter, cutting pulp, cedar pole, and a few logs. The lumbering was done on a much smaller scale than in our old district. The lumbermen returned home every night instead of camping out in the woods.

The life of these lumbermen differed greatly from that of the so-called lumberjacks who left home early in the fall and remained in the woods until late spring. In my stay at Umsaskis we had had the opportunity to visit several families in which the husband was away in the woods almost the year round. Invariably they were large families and the wife lived contentedly with the children while her husband labored away from home and sent her his monthly pay. I was amazed at the good homes these people had. There are always exceptions, of course. The lumberjack of the old days was known as a rough character who worked industriously the year round, saving his money so that when the time came that the logging drive closed, he could go to some big town or city and squander everything he had earned on one

Annette Jackson, 1950.

big blowout, on firewater and palefaces. Then after a few weeks, broke and fed up with life in a town, he returned to the deep woods and began another cycle.

After a few years my husband reported a great increase of game in his district. Deer trails which for many years had been abandoned were now beaten down again by large herds of deer. Frequently he saw deer browsing. I suppose I would have a hard time proving it, but I firmly believe that the increase in game and fish hereabouts is largely the result of Dave's energetic patrolling. Poachers and other violators have been severely dealt with. And the fish and game, given a fighting chance, have multiplied proportionately. Tracking down poachers is one of the most difficult aspects of the warden's job. Poachers are wily, smart operators who are willing to go to crazy lengths to outwit the law. If the warden is a little wilier, a little smarter, and just as willing to suffer hardships, the poacher is sent on the run.

Once while Dave was making an inspection trip along the border where he knew some poaching was going on, he left a lumber camp very early in the morning in search of two poachers he had heard about who had been in the territory for several days. He soon came upon fresh tracks which he followed a few miles, not certain that they were the right ones. As it turned out these were only the tracks of a lumber inspector. However, while returning, he came across two fresh sets of tracks. He decided to follow them for a ways. Toward the end of the afternoon, as he reached the edge of a swamp to which the tracks led, he heard the voices of two men talking French. As Dave approached he saw that they were in the act of gutting a deer. Near them a rifle leaned against a tree. Dave maneuvered himself silently around in such a way that he was able to grab the rifle just at the instant when one of the men spotted him. The other, seeing his partner turn white with fear, whirled around, lunged for the rifle, and shouted, "I keel you!" There was a brief tussle, which ended as suddenly as it had begun. The two French-Canadians all at once took to their heels, plunged into the swamp, and left Dave with the deer carcass and the rifle. Dave never saw hide nor hair of the two poachers again until a few years later when one of them wanted to come here to work. He asked my husband if he was still subject to a fine. If he was, he said, he would pay it, for during all the years which had passed since the scuffle with Dave he had been afraid to cross over the border.

Dave very seldom talks about his experiences, but I remember very well that he returned from one of his many trips with a small hole in his hat. It was without question a bullet hole. The many miles of Canadian border which he had to cover were miles of experience, miles of hardship, miles of adventure.

During the month of December one year a Canadian bomber crashed in the East Lake region. Dave offered his help in the search for the five airmen who had bailed out of the plane. He was put in charge of a search party of five hundred men to hunt for one of the crew who had not been found. The search took place in the deepest wilderness country in the state in extremely cold weather. For many days it stayed below zero, getting down some nights as low as forty and fifty degrees below. The search party spent days hunting for the lost pilot. All the others had been found at once, but the pilot never showed up alive. His body was found during the spring in a small brook. Apparently he had stooped to drink and because of his weakness and injuries was unable to get up again. Nearby Dave found a note stuck into the bark of a tree with the pin of his wings. He had written:

It's Cheerio, lads. It was fun while it lasted and none of you
have had the fun. I jumped overboard a few minutes ago and I'm
going to try to make it. You'll find my watch in my breast pocket.

Send it to my girl in Halifax. Write a letter to my mother and explain how it all happened.

To this he had signed his name.

The original settlers of this plantation came from Fredricton and St. John at the mouth of the St. John River. Some came from the Restigouche region and others from the St. Lawrence. These people were not young when they established themselves here. Undergoing many hardships, they poled up the St. John River in birch-bark canoes, pirogues, and laplands. The pirogue canoe was hollowed out of a pine log about twenty feet in length. After the log was dug out to a certain thickness, the bark was peeled off and both ends were tapered. The lapland was another variation of the pirogue. Living only on fish and caribou meat and sourdough bread for months at a time, the early settlers had a tough go of it. But they were a strong, determined, not easily discouraged lot and they hung on until they succeeded in fighting a living out of the countryside.

The Gardners, Kellys, McBriartys, Walkers, Haffords, Jacksons, and Pelkeys were the people who first ventured miles up this river. The forest was untamed then by any human being. The only trails through the woods were the ones made by bears, caribou, and other animals. The Gardners were the first to settle down. They chose a large island for their home, built a cabin to accommodate their family, and started farming. Soon others ventured farther up the river, choosing places which appealed to them. Year by year land was cleared away. Before long there was a road over which teams of horses could travel to the nearest village more than a hundred miles away.

Some of the first settlers were far-sighted enough to bring potatoes with them. Before eating the potatoes they would remove the eyes and sow them in little hills fertilized with fish. Thus in a sense they could eat their potatoes and have them, too.

The ability of these old-timers to get along with what they had at hand fills me with admiration. My father once told me how they made soap by reducing animal fats to grease, boiling wood ashes to get lye, and combining the grease and ash water in a brew which they boiled with a certain amount of melted spruce gum. After several hours of boiling, the mixture would be allowed to cool and harden and was then cut into chunks. It made a very good soap, light in color.

I ate my first sourdough bread after I came here to Allagash, where generation after generation had learned to do this kind of baking. It is delicious and light, but I have yet to get up enough courage to attempt to make a batch of it myself. There is a lot more to it than there is to so-called fancy bread-making.

Gradually I adapted myself to living in this small community and to the new way of life. I was most kindly received by our schoolteachers and a number of other ladies. I was invited to take part in certain school programs and gatherings. For three years I drove a group of ten children to the biggest school, ten miles away. The drive took about half an hour, a good part of which we would spend singing. Some of the children were very good singers. Although they'd had no vocal training at all, their little voices were clear and soft and true.

I was elected to the school board and appointed truant officer. All this was completely new and interesting to me. However, I soon found out how difficult it was to maintain good attendance in our schools. With the help of our teachers I was able to succeed in some cases. But many of the parents were not willing to lend a hand. A little reading, writing, and arithmetic had been good enough for them, and by golly, it was going to be good enough for their children. Furthermore, their knowing ancestors had gotten along pretty well without even being able to write their own names! The fight against such an attitude was sometimes quite difficult, but fortunately most parents in Allagash Plantation cooperated very heartily. Many spent a great deal of hard-earned money for the education of their sons and daughters. Most wished for and did everything possible to better the schools.

During my three years as a member of the school board I had an opportunity to learn a great deal about our school system and the meager funds available to it. The first little school of the Allagash Plantation was built on Gardner Island at the mouth of the Allagash River. By that time enough families had settled on the island and on the banks of the St. John to justify erecting a school. As the families increased and more people moved into the untamed woodland along the rivers, the forests became alive with the sounds of chopping and the falling of large timbers. More people moved farther up the river, and as time went by the farms became larger. People lived simply. They farmed and hunted and fished and trapped. And then years later the lumbering company bought and took over this great timberland. It deeded to each of the settlers the few acres of land he had settled on. The community grew. Although farming continued, lumbering became the big thing.

A team road to Fort Kent, the nearest town, was built. In later years a car road has been built and a general store added, but somehow the Plantation never seems to have developed as other towns have. Generation after generation have clung to the homes of their ancestors, living the same way, making few changes or improvements. Today, men ferry themselves across the river just as their ancestors did a hundred years ago, pulling themselves across by means of a cable.

Many of the farms which used to be large and prosperous are now overgrown with fir and spruce and alder. Soon they will be forest once again. Yet even so, the area thrives in a small way. Some of the young men and girls have married people from other towns, yet the couples have returned here to make their homes in the old homesteads. There are still big families here, and people seem to live to a ripe old age.

The most exciting day of the year in the Allagash Plantation comes in March when the annual town meeting takes place.

People young and old who otherwise never stir themselves, as well as all the normally active citizens, attend Town Meeting. In this area as in all others there are busy little cliques combating one another, each doing its utmost to force its own favorite slate of candidates into office. The meeting takes place in one of the five schoolhouses. The ladies gather on one side, the men on the other. In the center is the teacher's desk and chair. Books are still on her desk.

Once the town clerk walks in, the meeting is under way. The town clerk, a lady in her fifties, has held her position for thirty years and knows very well all that goes on. She comes in with her records (birth certificates and so forth) packed in a paper box which she deposits on the floor beside her. She calls for silence in the room, and a moderator is chosen and approved by a show of hands. Warrant in hand, he steps forward and stands beside the town clerk. He looks very nervous. The paper shakes in his hand.

Now the town clerk sits down. She is a plump, white-haired woman, a little flushed with excitement. She wears her spectacles on the tip of her nose and is ready for a busy evening. A big book is open on the desk in front of her and, pencil in hand,

she sits ready to start entering in it a record of the evening's pro-
ceedings. She will have a lot of writing to do. This plantation
is rich. Wild-land taxes and other taxes provide something like
ninety-five thousand dollars, the disposition of which is to be
discussed at this meeting. The town clerk is here to see that no
mistakes are made in budgeting it.

The First Selectman is elected. There are smiles of triumph
on the faces of the winner and his supporters, and grimaces of
disappointment on the faces of the losers. Then a second selectman and finally the third are elected. Appropriations for the
town roads, the poor, and the school systems are made. There
are not many things left to vote on, but many arguments begin.

"A discussion of the roads is most important," someone says.
"What about the Rapid Road? Last year you said there wasn't
enough money, and it went unrepaired. The road is so bad you
can barely go over it with a truck or a team of horses. There
wasn't a shovelful of gravel put on it last year. What are you
going to do about it?"

"This has been going on for years," another shouts. "The first
thing you know there won't be any roads left. Mr. Selectman,
what are you going to do about it?"

Mr. Selectman gets very cross and red in the face. He replies,
"We will do our best this year."

But the people know it will be the same as last year: not
enough money.

Someone way back in the corner of the room shouts, "What
about Frank McBriarty's road? It's so bad everyone gets stuck on
it. That should be fixed too."

He gets the same reply. And the reply is sadly familiar to
everyone present. It is one that has been repeated for years at
these annual meetings . . . "We will do our best."

Later comes a discussion of money for our schoolteachers. Year after year one of the childless citizens is sure to start to argue.

"We always vote too much money for schools. The teachers needn't be paid so much. They don't work any too hard."

The discussion gets warm, with people chiming in from all parts of the room, and finally a small additional amount is voted for the schools. The Plantation's schools are in such disrepair that they are usable only during the warm months.

The next and most important item is money to be voted for the poor. Too often at these meetings someone asks the overseer of the poor to read off the names of those who required help last year.

"This selectman," someone in the crowd says, "was so good to the poor last year that their votes are sure to reelect him this year."

Over five thousand dollars is voted for relief.

One in the group says, "Hmmmm . . . it's funny I couldn't get a cent of that money. Yet a few of the people who get it are riding around the Plantation in their own cars, running their own outboards, going off on leisurely fishing trips . . ."

The town has to content itself with only two ferryboats. The man running them gets top pay, for his hours are long ones. The First Selectman standing in front of the room says two more bateaus will have to be built for use when it is impossible to use the ferryboats or when someone comes along after hours and the ferryman is off duty. But this stirs up opposition.

Someone shouts, "We built two last spring."

The selectman answers, "Sure, but the last one to cross just before the freeze-up didn't tie the bateau and it went adrift."

There are continued wranglings before the ninety-five thousand dollars are disposed of. Everyone has his say. One dissatisfied citizen even shouts, "Allagash is the richest plantation in the state and it is also the poorest-looking one."

The meeting is adjourned. Many stay to discuss what should be done and what should not be done. The lady town clerk, reelected, picks up her papers and is happy.

And so life goes on in our little community.

A few years after we moved into the Allagash territory the lumber companies operating here cut several roads through this section of the forest. These were needed both to haul supplies in to the cutters and to haul out the pulp and timber which they cut. Certainly the convenience of game wardens didn't enter into their thinking—but for Dave and his fellow wardens, these new roads were a blessing. They made it possible for him to visit by car many of the camps which previously had been accessible only by foot or by canoe.

Even so, winter travel over these third-grade roads is pretty miserable. At best a car is an undependable piece of machinery in temperatures which go as low as thirty-five and forty degrees below zero. On one occasion Dave rescued the Border Patrol from one of these unpreventable winter mishaps. He found them stranded on the Black River Road, where they had stopped to repair a mechanical defect of some sort. While they were trying to fix it the car froze up tight, and there remained the choice of staying with the car and freezing to death or of piling in with Dave and riding home with him. Needless to say, they went along. Just to complicate matters further, a heavy snowstorm began shortly after they arrived at our place, and as a result they didn't set eyes on their car again until the spring thaw set in and a team of horses was dispatched to haul it into town.

To picture what conditions are like in the woods during winter, city dwellers must recall the worst unpaved roads they have ever seen and then try to imagine what those roads would be like during the worst winter they have ever experienced. Perhaps the picture would be more accurate if after imagining this sorry scene they could somehow multiply it by two or three. They would then come close to approximating the standard winter conditions deep in the woods.

Despite the fierce changes in temperature, the brute strength of the storms which prevail in winter in these parts, and the apparent absence of any means of feeding themselves, the deer survive our winters without undue casualty. Their heavy tough hide and winter coat keep them warm. Like other animals they benefit by changes in their coloration which occur from season to season. And somehow—provided the winter isn't a particularly icy, sleety one—they manage to find enough moss and bark and sufficient small branches to feed themselves through the winter. Things are bad for them if heavy rains are frequent during the winter, for the low prevailing temperatures up here turn these to ice, and thick coats of ice on bark and branches and moss make feeding almost impossible. Then the herds thin out and many of the deer die.

Perhaps the worst enemy of the deer is the bobcat. He slinks about the forest following the herds during the winter, waiting craftily for one of the deer to fatten and drop behind. When one does, he falls upon it and destroys it. Rabbits and partridges are also victims of the bobcat's hunger. While I am, as I have said, afraid of bears, I think the bobcat is the most unpleasant animal abroad in these woods.

I had often heard Dave and some of the old trappers we encountered in our travels talk about deer licks, but I had never had the opportunity to see one until we stayed for a few days one fall during the hunting season at a lumber camp on Sweeney Brook. On our way back from an inspection of the cuttings one afternoon, Dave led me off the road and up an old deer trail so constantly trampled down that in places it was twenty inches deep. The trail led to a natural salt lick, a dark, damp patch of earth which for some reason or other has a salty taste. Here the deer stand and paw the earth to turn up saltier portions which they lick until their craving for salt is satisfied. Then, since Sweeney Brook is close by, they trot down to it, quench their thirst, and go on about their business.

The biggest deer lick in the state of Maine is in the far northern part of the state. It is an area six acres square and so thoroughly worked over by deer that in certain portions holes three feet deep have been dug by their frantic pawing.

Here you find the roots of trees exposed by the scrabbling of many deer. And you find also that because of the salty character of the earth the trees have assumed strange, gnarled shapes. As a matter of fact, the salt licks I have seen are in locations almost inaccessible to man. The low growth of trees and underbrush is generally so tangled that the deer themselves have some struggling to do to get to them. I have heard that it was not uncommon, back forty or more years ago, to see as many as fifty deer at once at the big deer lick up north. I love to sit a short distance from the deer lick and just watch, for I have great patience and never become discouraged. This outdoor life which I love so well took me back year after year to this same place.

Every day of hunting meant a lot to Dave and myself. We relive again and again the hearty breakfast each morning, the game we saw each day. We laugh over the old rope I always carried to haul my deer into camp and the bottle of vodka we always had along to treat friends. There are memories of the evenings in camp sitting before a warming campfire and of being hauled out of bed before dawn with Dave hollering, "You're hunting today, old girl. You've got to get your buck. Come on, you can sleep after you've shot him."

Those hunting trips—they'll never be forgotten.

Arriving one night at Glazier very late, we paddled by moonlight across this three-mile-wide lake. The moon was so bright one could read by its light. In the far distance we could hear a radio playing sweet music, and across the lake, on the Canadian side of the border, some fishermen were tented for the night and keeping a campfire. We kept paddling until we came to McPherson Pond, where the game warden's camp is situated. The little camp is built so close to the shore of this pond that on a rise of water its floor gets wet. The camp was built by some of the wardens who had worked in the area before my husband's transfer. Looking over the surroundings the next morning I found that I liked the location. The ridges were untouched by the lumbermen, deer and other game were plentiful, and the battle with the salmon and trout was enjoyed by fishermen who came from miles away.

After a breakfast of fried trout and coffee we set out for Beau Lake, twenty miles farther along. This is an interesting journey, for it takes you about as far north as it is possible to go and still remain in the eastern United States. A little north of where we were is the northernmost tip of the state of Maine. On the Canadian side of Beau Lake are the provinces of Quebec and New Brunswick. There are pleasant farms to be seen there, though on our side of the lake most of the land is still covered by forests of fir, pine, and hardwood.

We cooked a late dinner on the shore in front of the game warden's camp at Beau Lake. We ate outside for the simple reason that the last occupants had failed to close the door when they left and the porcupines had taken over. The camp is built on stilts high up from the ground about two hundred feet from the water's edge and has a wide porch in front. One may sit and listen to a bubbling brook which empties into the lake and runs continuously all summer long. The surrounding mountains are beautiful with their bright coloring in the fall. A path beaten down by the deer leads up the mountain back of the camp through a rich growth of maple, beech, and tamarack. Bears were plentiful, and traveling through the woods we saw many signs of them.

When game is thick in the timberland, if you are a good woodsman, you can easily tell almost to the exact number how many deer, bear, and other kinds of game roam the surrounding country. The Department of Fish and Game has trained a man in this sort of work, and once every few years a census is taken to determine the amount of game at large. Without special training it is possible for a woodsman to make fairly respectable guesses about the animal population of the area he lives in. After a few seasons in the woods, you recognize the signs.

Bears, for example, frequently tear apart fallen trees which are rotten from age and weather. Inside they find thousands of small ants which they delight in eating. More out of playfulness than hunger, they also strip small fir trees of their limbs and bark. Raise your eyes a bit and you spot the evidence buck deer frequently leave behind them. Six or eight feet up you see broken limbs on a small birch here and there. This means that the buck has hooked his antlers in the limbs and yanked the limbs apart trying to disentangle himself. Deer follow the same trails year after year, and over the course of time some of these trails become so thoroughly beaten down that it is impossible even for the unobservant to miss them. Follow them and they lead you to the thickest part of the timberland, to swamps and lowlands, to hidden springs, brooks, and streams.

Out back of the camp at Beau Lake there is a steep hill up which there runs a deer trail that leads to the top of the ridge. Several years ago my husband was following this little trail when he noticed that the ground to one side of the trail broke away as he put his weight on it. He thought nothing of it, but as seasons passed he realized that here was a real landslide in the making: The side of this cliff was imperceptibly falling away. Today it is no longer possible for us to climb to the old trail—though if you stand down on the lakeshore you can still see it on the very top edge of the cliff.

Waterways, too, undergo many changes without one's noticing. During the fall of one year Dave and I were returning from Blue River. Just as we came in view of Beau Lake, Dave spotted a man on the high bank of a little island at the mouth of the river. Thinking that he was hunting, he stopped to check his license. He paddled over to the shore, beached the canoe, and after climbing up to the top of the bank, asked the man to show him his license.

The man acted greatly surprised. He said, "I don't need a license."

Dave said, "What! You don't need a license to hunt?"

The man clutching at his rifle suddenly realized that the warden was speaking English. He said, "Warden, I tink you are mistaking. Dis is on Canada."

Dave did a double-take. "Canada?" he said. "How come? Since when?"

The man then explained how the flow of water had changed its course and cut through the mainland, thus making an island which was about two acres square. This island on which Dave and the hunter stood was really a little piece of the Canadian mainland and the hunter had gone there to get a shot at some ducks he had spotted.

Dave returned to the canoe with a grin on his face, and without saying a word backtracked to the mouth of the river and began to investigate in order to find the actual channel of this late change. He found it, all right, and he also found that there were other places where the flow of water had made similarly curious changes.

We talked a good deal about these and other changes, and Dave told me of Fifth Lake Musquacook which in 1927 had been a good-sized lake with good fishing. Then it began to fill with vegetation, and only a few years later it was completely covered over except for one small area of open water. The rest is now a growth of bog bushes and bog spruce.

Fall Brook Lake seems to be destined for the same fate as Fifth Lake Musquacook, for what used to be a deep basin of water with a muddy bottom that could not be reached with a twenty-foot pole is now a shallow body of water the bottom of which can easily be seen. All around the margins of the lake now there is nothing but a growth of bog bushes and many bog spruce. In years to come, no doubt, youngsters will listen with an air of tolerant amusement when old-timers tell about the good old days fishing in Fall Brook Lake.

The waters of Fall Brook Lake empty into a small brook which flows east, and after many twistings and turnings through quick water and dead water ends up with a forty-foot fall into the St. Francis River. Many times I have accompanied my husband on night trips in this area. Often we have tented on the trail near Fall Brook and looked over across the St. Francis River at the small farm there. It is a very pleasant place. In the early morning the scenery is restful and beautiful, and to wake up to the sound of a cowbell in the pasture nearby, and later to listen to the humming of motors coming up the river is an experience which I find combines pleasurable feelings of isolation and companionship.

Fall Brook Lake is a natural trout hatchery. More trout have been taken from this lake than from any other in the state of Maine. Hundreds of fishermen spend their weekends here fishing. The trout vary little in size and do not run very large. But the flesh of these trout is a dark pink; they are fat and most tasty, and when a fisherman gets one on the end of his line, he knows he's in for some hectic excitement.

Frequently during the summer we have taken trips on the Little Black River. Because of its endless variety it is one of my favorites. One may go by outboard as far as thirty miles up the river. The water is always fair and the going is easy. I loved especially to go in early June, when you find the banks so covered with fiddlehead ferns that you would think they were being cultivated.

The Little Black River is not very large, about two hundred feet wide at its widest. The banks are high along most of its length. Here and there are low sandy points. The water, deep and black, mirrors the sky and the trees along the banks so brilliantly that you have the feeling that you are floating away in midair. It is a curious feeling to look down over the side of your boat and see a bird flying away beneath you.

The Little Black River differs from the other rivers hereabouts in that it twists and zigzags crazily through the timberland. Sometimes, looking back, you have the feeling that you just went around an island, because you can see water almost all about the spit of land you have just paddled by. But it is only one of the Little Black's numberless backtracks which seem to lead nowhere.

If you have never seen beavers at work you have missed something very interesting. With their amazing teeth they fell trees fifteen to twenty inches in diameter. And they make them fall precisely where they want them to fall, on top of one another. They then nibble off the branches and store them away for the winter. Like other timber workers, beavers sometimes get involved in accidents. I recall a trapper coming to our place once with a beaver that he had found crushed under a big poplar tree. Some of the old trappers insist that there are such things as lazy beavers and that when other members of a beaver family discover that a certain one is goldbricking, they expel him and send him off to get along by himself.

The St. John River, known to some as the Maine River, is a legend in itself. The source of the St. John is near the Canadian border, at which point it is no more than a step wide. As it flows farther down, it widens gradually until, by the time it empties into the Bay of Fundy, it is a very large river. A good many years ago when lumbermen were driving square timber logs, the drivers were obstructed by some huge rocks in the river. These were blown to smithereens by dynamite, and a passable channel was thus gouged out. The remains of some of these rocks, looking like stacks of hay, can still be seen at the head of the river.

I have spent many a day on the St. John River and many more on its banks, hunting, fishing, and wandering around enjoying the views, and I have come to have a deep respect for this stretch of water. In one day's passage you encounter just about everything a river has to offer: fast water, dead water, small and large rapids. The beauty of the great valley through which the St. John runs, the spectacle of mountains in the distance, and the pleasing variety provided by the many little brooks which empty into the river combine to make a trip on her worthwhile in every way.

When you leave Allagash to begin the trip upriver, you encounter a roaring rapid with three bad drops. Within the space of three miles the level falls seventy feet. The going here is very difficult and only the foolhardy or the highly skilled undertake the run. Since Dave belongs to the latter category, I have ridden these rapids with him many times, always, I might add, without fear—and with never a mishap.

In placid water, with Dave handling the outboard, I frequently pass the time lolling back on cushions on the bottom of the canoe, reading. Now and then it is fun to look up from my book and see how the prospect has changed—we are coursing through woodland now; just a chapter ago we were floating through low open meadow land—that sort of thing. Occasionally we see that we have company in the water. A deer or a mink plunges in to swim to the other side in one of the mysterious errands animals go on. A squirrel swims toward the canoe. And I have found, time and again, that if I put a paddle in the water and extend it toward the squirrel, he will scramble up onto the paddle and jump into the canoe.

Against Dave's advice one day, I caught one of these little fellows with my bare hands. I got my fingers well bitten with little teeth as sharp as needles. Nevertheless, on that occasion I did manage to capture and cage the little squirrel and we kept him at home for the children for several weeks. He was just a little ball of fat, fur, and teeth, with lively, round little eyes.

Generally on our trips down the St. John we stay the night at a little camp at the foot of the Big Black Rapids about a mile from where the Big Black River empties into the St. John. This little camp was built by a trapper who later turned it over to the Fish and Game Department for the use of the warden. Like all trappers' cabins it is small, tidy, and extremely simple.

Big Black Rapid is one of the most thrilling stretches of fast water in this region. It is a mile long and it takes only three minutes to cover the distance in a canoe. A mile of roaring white water spotted here and there with partly covered rocks, it is no place for a novice. I have seen men come down it with their outboards down, but paddling seems much saner to Dave and me. I have put some pretty heavy wear on the gunwales of our canoe, clutching for all I was worth as we rode these rapids at different times. It is a breathtaking ride.

On one of our trips a few years ago, we went through these rapids five times, chugging up the rapids each time with our outboard and later, paddling down. The ride down was alarming the first couple of times, but I got used to it and dared on the last couple of trips down to take my eyes off the water and watch the evergreens and the sky go whirling away behind us.

In conversations about the rapids I had heard mention of stairs. After these trips up and down, I knew what people were talking about. The stairs are irregular rock ledges which extend twenty or more feet into the river from the shore on both sides.

Back at home my time was divided between trips into the timberland and on the rivers with my husband and taking care of our children and our household. The summers fly by all too quickly to suit me, and before we knew it all three of our children were in school. The schoolhouse was only a step away from our house, yet even so Arlene didn't want to go, and the first few days we had to carry her there bodily. She was a very shy child. Robert and Hilda, however, took school very seriously and went to it willingly.

Our way of living did not change in any important way after the transfer. It did seem to me that we were all getting old too quickly. That thought had never occurred to me when we were settled in our fixed routine at Umsaskis. But the move was a

little unsettling, and for a while prompted such musings. I loved
the wilderness so much and I missed the feeling of closeness to it
which we had had back at Umsaskis. Nevertheless, the unrolling
of the seasons continued to be a source of endless pleasure for
me. I found one as pleasurable as the next, and I still wonder
when I hear people say they have a favorite season. I still wonder
when I hear people say, for instance, that winter is harsh and
summer is genial. In my estimation, each moment of the year
has its own beauty and each moment is wonderfully different
from the ones which precede and follow it. The change in the
surroundings give a different aspect from month to month. The
tribes of birds and the insects and the endless varieties of plants
all have their own strange punctuality. They flourish on time and
they move along to make room for others crowding to follow.
I make a quick roster of the things in Nature that particularly delight me, and I shudder at the thought of a new calendar
which might eliminate any one of the year's gorgeous seasons.
Dewy mornings, rainbows, blossoming trees, trees hooded with
snow, the stars, moonlight, shadows in the still water, the earth
carpeted with fallen leaves—all these lovely things, and so many
more, are needed to make a year.

Chapter 18

Time Marches On

A few times since our move from Umsaskis I have gone back to visit our old camp. The changes seem tremendous. In a strange way it disturbs me now on these infrequent returns to my old haunts to find that things are not what they were. I have certain pictures fixed in my memory, and it is oddly discomforting to find that my memory and present-day facts are so dissimilar. Today when I sit in what used to be my favorite retreat on the banks of the lake, I can no longer see the little cove with the deep-blue water up by the head of the lake. The growth of foliage has been so dense as to blot it completely out of view. The little maple we planted when we first moved into the cabin is now huge enough to tower and throw its cool shade over the camp, garage and all. The camp is deserted, and the path to our spring is covered by untrampled moss. And the garden which Dave spent so much time spading and fencing in is a tangle of high grass, weeds, and bushes.

So life goes. We get in the habit of thinking that personally we remain pretty much unchanged despite the years. How wrong we are. Still, a look at the surroundings where one lived in his youth is somehow much more revealing of the ravages of time than the mirror one looks in every day.

In 1943 David, our fourth child, was born. He was less of a problem than the others had been—largely because by the time he came along, Hilda and Robert and Arlene were well grown and self-reliant children. More than that, they were good, helpful children, so that I not only had all the time I needed to take care of the new baby, but I also had three stalwart helpers to give me a hand when I needed it. It seemed no time before David was through with formula, bottles, and afternoon naps and ready to toddle off to school. Now, at eleven, he is a little image of his father. Although he shows no great fondness for extended trips through the woods, he insists that he is going to be a game warden when he grows up. And looking back over the many happy years Dave and I spent together in the woods, I am sure he could choose a worse way of spending his life.

Robert is now old enough to be awaiting his call to the army. While I dislike the idea of having his life interrupted and of having him separated from us for so long a time, this is one of those things that every family must undergo these days. In a way I suppose military discipline is a good thing for young men. In another way, however, I keep wishing we lived in a world where there would be no need for armies. Even so, Robert will get along without any difficulty. Considering his age he has held more jobs, more varied jobs, than anyone I ever heard of. He's a good tinkerer, the sort of person who with the tools and equipment at hand can do a better job than many others could if they had Sears, Roebuck's warehouse at their disposal.

Hilda is about to finish high school, after which she will go into a training school for nurses. She is a tiny girl, blonde and petite and very good to look at. I feel sure she'll be a good nurse, for not only is her heart in the right place, but she is also tidy, methodical, and efficient.

Arlene, our oldest, is tall and handsome and filled with ambition. She is a teacher now and if her dreams come true, she'll head for Alaska one of these days to continue her teaching in a wilderness area denser even than this.

Bringing up four children on a game warden's salary has been a never-ending process of making silk purses out of sows' ears. Dave and I have managed it by doing ourselves many of the things that people generally hire others to do. Dave has been carpenter, plumber, painter; I, tailor, dressmaker, farmer, canner. By our own efforts and with the outlay of as little cash as possible, we have managed to keep ourselves and our children adequately housed, clothed, fed, and content. At various times we have supplemented our income by making dry flies and selling them to fishermen, by taking part in the annual potato harvest, and—for a while, at least—by taking in roomers and boarders. In recent years the older children have been able to help out, and they have done so as a matter of course.

Far be it from me to suggest that Dave and I are getting to be fogies. Nevertheless, it is a fact that for one reason or another we are not as active as we used to be. It is almost four years since our last extended hunting trip together, back in November 1950.

In raw, cold weather that time we set out for the warden's camp on the Big Black. We found it empty, tidied it up, got a roaring fire going, and spent a happy evening together reminiscing. Next day, a Sunday, Dave had to spend most of the daylight hours on his official rounds. I slept late, breakfasted in leisurely fashion, and then sat down to read while awaiting his return. While he was still away another pair of hunters arrived and asked if they could share the camp. They were, of course, welcome. It was evening before Dave got back, and since we planned to get out early next morning to look for our deer, we turned in shortly after supper.

Dave routed me out of bed at the crack of dawn. We had a quick breakfast and then piled into the canoe and paddled to Steward Brook. There we discovered that a bear had torn the tarpaper off the roof of the cabin and Dave felt obliged to stop to repair that damage. While this was going on I waited around uneasily, fearful that the bear might show up again while we were there. It didn't, and Dave and I were soon on our way again.

We paddled through the Big Black Rapid, and it was thrilling to feel the canoe cutting through the foaming white water while fine spray whipped up by a brisk breeze cut at my face. This was sheer enjoyment now, for I no longer had any fear of the rapids. At the head we pulled the canoe up onto dry land and hiked inland a way to scout along an old tote road. We saw plenty of fresh deer tracks but no deer, and then, while Dave went on ahead to have a look at a brook which he knew beavers were attempting to dam, I walked back to the canoe and sat on the shore, keeping my eyes peeled for any sign of movement which might mean deer. No luck. By the time Dave returned the first hints of dusk were beginning to become apparent.

We got in the canoe and headed back to camp. As we approached the foot of the rapid, I spotted a small object on the shore about half a mile away. It was a deer. As we came nearer we saw that it was a huge buck with a tremendous set of horns. I wanted Dave to shoot it, but he insisted that I take the shot. There was no time for discussion. The deer had moved to the water's edge—his large set of horns extended on each side of his head, his broad chest and shoulder completely exposed—a perfect target. I took aim and fired. With a high jump and a wave of his white tail, the buck disappeared into the woods nearby.

I turned to Dave. He stood, stunned.

"My God!" he said when he came to. "That deer would have taken first prize in the big buck club at Allagash, and the kit is better than one hundred and seventeen dollars—not even considering the meat."

I was in tears. It had been such a perfect target. I could not believe I had missed.

When Dave asked me where I had aimed, I told him I had fired at the shoulder. Putting the tow rope and the rifle down in the bow of the canoe, we started walking toward the spot where the deer had stood. I couldn't see the tracks, so I returned to the canoe while Dave continued the search. He wouldn't give up.

Twenty minutes later he returned to the canoe and asked for my rope. I looked at him thinking that he was teasing me, for he had chided me at my insistence on carrying my rope to tow the deer I might get. But I gave him the rope, and stumbling along to keep up with his steps, I began to wonder if I had gotten my buck.

Twenty feet from the edge of the wood where he had been standing when I shot at him lay the deer. He was an eight-point buck with identical horns. His throat was a snowy white and his fur thick and clean. I was thrilled beyond speech.

Dave and I examined the deer and found that he had been hit an inch back of the shoulder. The bullet had cut the top part of the liver, and the blood had remained inside. The lack of blood was what had made the deer so difficult to track. I helped as much as I could and we hauled the deer to the canoe—our guess was that he weighed about two hundred pounds. It was nearly dark when we reached camp, and as I climbed the bank to the cabin I shouted to the couple who were sharing it with us. They rushed out to admire my catch.

We had fresh deer liver for dinner that night, and Dave brought out the last of the vodka, which is a traditional celebration for the first deer killed in camp. I was also to have the privilege of sleeping late in the morning. The moon was bright that evening and several times I stole out to admire my buck. After a night filled with beautiful dreams of hunting magnificent deer, I awakened to a bright sunny day. The snow had melted some the day before, the weather was warm, and for hunters the woods would be perfect. Even though my hunt was over, we were to stay in the vicinity of Big Black for four more days.

Dave had many hunters to check along the river, and the four days passed quickly. On the morning of the fifth day we loaded our luggage and my beautiful deer and headed for home. It was a magnificent morning, warm and clear. Though the water was at a good height, we decided to paddle. The snow was gone and the bare ground was once again exposed.

Though it was the last day of November I thought of it as a patch of Indian summer. Most of the ducks and geese had migrated, but there were still a few who would remain through the winter. The bare trees did not mar the beauty of the surrounding ridges. It did not seem possible that in a few weeks, winter would be at its icy work again, the forests deep in snow, and thick ice on the rivers, lakes, and brooks. Boys and men on the faraway farms would be going up the slopes to tap the sugar maples. Then March, half lamb and half lion, would rush in on a blustering wind, with the nights still zero cold and snowstorms thicker than any yet seen. But its warm rain would break the winter, and when the gray folds of the sky were swept away, a warmth would be felt in the streaming sun.

As we neared home, my thoughts turned to our future. Dave's twenty-five years as a Fish and Game warden would soon be over. We would have new experiences and new adventures. The head of my prized deer I would mount and hang in our sitting room—a wonderful reminder of our time together, of the wilderness we loved and shared, and the enchantment of its waters that had somehow spread itself into our life together.

Epilogue

Thirty-Two Years Later: Back to the River

The fog was lifting on the St. John River when we left the Jalbert Tourist Home. As we bid Mrs. Jalbert good-bye, I settled on the seat between my husband and the "Old Guide."

It was an early August morning during the mid-1960s. I felt a twinge of excitement and the palms of my hands were damp. I, too, was going on this famous trip, which was called the Telos River trip. And I realized it was my first trip in parts of this region and perhaps my last. I was assigned to cook for the entire trip, for the guides and the two ladies whom they were going to guide. We were to meet at Shin Pond, in the northern part of Maine.

It gave the appearance of becoming a beautiful day. The hills and the countryside unrolled ahead of us, making way to a beautiful morning.

The pickup loaded with all our equipment for a ten-day trip rolled smoothly over the distance at the usual normal speed.

It was midday when we arrived at Shin Pond. The two ladies, Mrs. Brown and Dr. Freese—whom the Old Guide later on during the trip called "Mrs. Doctor"—were standing in the doorway of the hotel. The Old Guide, who favors the ladies, looked sort of happy while I whispered out of the corner of my mouth, "Which is your pick?"

He nudged me with his elbow, and with a grin on his face, I watched him shaking hands with the ladies. My husband and I were introduced to them, I as the cook, and my husband, the second guide.

Dave suggested that I ride the balance of the way with them in their car to keep them informed of what was ahead.

We realized the two ladies were strange to the ways of the wilderness, and it appeared they were somewhat nervous to be so far away in the backwoods.

Mrs. Brown was a perfect driver, and soon we arrived at the landing where the equipment was unloaded and sorted for each canoe. I was still wondering which one the Old Guide would choose. He chose "Mrs. Doctor." I was also going to share the same canoe. Dave would be with Mrs. Brown.

On such a trip my style of traveling is very simple, yet very efficient. I carry a beach-bag of waterproof material with a pretty design. In it goes half a dozen pieces of underwear, a pair of warm pajamas, two pairs of socks, one spare pair of slacks of light woolen material (never dungarees or cotton ones), one long-sleeved shirt, one woolen shirt which I carry with me outside of the bag, one pair of camp leather sleepers, one towel, and toilet articles, just enough for the trip, in plastic containers.

In my field glasses' case, goes a washcloth, a small piece of soap, one bottle of nail polish, nail file, one small book of flies, fly dope, a silk kerchief, one small comb, a few pins, and my Kodak. I keep my field glasses by my side at all times, so that I can see the small animals along the shore.

Though I am considered a very good sportswoman, and someone who can get meals as well on an outdoor fireplace as on the fanciest stove, I never paddle or pole a canoe. My husband never expected it of me. Therefore, I enjoy the scenery, I read, do my nails, and write.

My husband's equipment is as limited as my own, plus the sleeping bags and my never-to-be-parted-from wool-spun blanket. The tent and two air mattresses complete our needs for a good fishing trip.

As in the old days, if the weather permits, I like to just unroll our sleeping bags and sleep right out under the sky. We choose a level spot not far from the fireplace, put the two mattresses together, put one sleeping bag over them, followed by my wool-spun blanket with the other sleeping bag on top, thus making a Waldorf Astoria bed out in the great open. I like tents only on stormy days, or to get out of the rain. Therefore, I intended to do just that during our trip.

Once the pickup was unloaded and the equipment sorted into each canoe, I was amazed to see the load we were carrying— food for ten days, a large duffel bag with the cooking dishes, plus the duffels for the two ladies, fishing gear, and sleeping bags. We had a trainload. Their duffels were far different from mine, weighing just about eighty pounds each, outside of the small bags they were carrying. I presumed to myself they needed it all to keep house.

Nevertheless, everything was loaded, Mrs. Doctor settled in the bow, and I settled back of the load in the stern, two feet from the guide. With the load in the center, I could not see a thing ahead. We took the lead, with Dave following, every one but me paddling. I noticed at my side a paddle, but I ignored it. It was still a beautiful afternoon, only the wind was more than a breeze and was stirring up the water to a rather undesirable wave, which the guides regarded as unimportant. I went along with that and settled deeper in my chair, taking stock of my trip ahead.

I wanted to make sure I would get as much enjoyment on this trip as if I were paying a small fortune for it. I was in the midst of daydreaming when I felt the Old Guide poking me on the shoulder.

"Paddle," he said. I glanced at him and shook my head, no. From my position it was very difficult to paddle, unless it happened to be a have-to.

After leaving the bridge which crosses the foot of Telos, we followed a thoroughfare, then into a small pond. By then the lake was churning badly, so when we got into Chamberlain Lake it was quite interesting. The Old Guide hitched Dave's canoe behind his in a manner that it was easily hauled, as we carried only one outboard motor on such a trip. We passed by several nice camping grounds, but they were occupied, so we went along, looking for the next best one.

Chamberlain Lake, which is the largest in the Allagash country, has a long spread, and often it is too rough to try to cross it, so one must hole up at one of the camping grounds somewhere along the lake.

That was what was happening to us. Dave and the Old Guide planned to make Alice Brook camping ground our destination instead of trying to cross Chamberlain Lake. Once we reached the cove, all would be fine, I was told.

Dave and Mrs. Brown were coming along back of us. However, loaded as we were, every wave hit them face-on and they were taking water. Mrs. Brown was getting wet in spite of the raincoat she wore.

We finally reached Alice Brook, and once in the cove, you had a feeling that the past half-hour was only a dream. All was calm there. The sun was warm and everyone seemed happy. Needless to say, in crossing Chamberlain in this manner, one misses much. I wished we could have come up the other side where we could have visited the old farmland which was left uncultivated for so many years.

This was to be my first supper; I had already planned what to cook, if I could find what I needed. I soon learned in order to find what I needed meant to investigate all boxes, while the tents were being put up, and the ladies were getting settled. I chose to have beefsteak this first evening, as the more perishable food had

Photo courtesy of Arlene Packard

Annette Jackson.

to be used up first. I made a salad, one yellow and one green veg-
etable, mashed potatoes, and hot biscuits.

I set the table nicely, with oilcloth, and everything else we
needed to make the meal complete. I had requested the Old
Guide bring along a nine-by-twelve polyester cloth that I wished
to use to cover the table after it was set. I put a small rock on
each corner of the table to keep the cloth from blowing away,
and thus keep the table neat and free from spills and flies. Dave
supplied the wood and the fire. All went well, and everyone was
happy over the meal.

With great hope of catching enough trout for breakfast,
everyone except myself went for the evening fishing. I remained
with my cooking equipment, making ready for the next day.

Once everything was sorted and stored in the right boxes, it seemed easy enough to put out a meal quickly.

When the party returned at dusk, there were no trout. It proved to be the same thing the following day, and the day after. Therefore, we would have a breakfast of bacon, eggs, and pancakes with maple syrup.

It was a clear day when the Old Guide hollered, "Turn-n-n ou-t-t!" at four the next morning. It wasn't my style, for when Dave and I went on the river, we waited until the fog was up, so that we could look over the entire lake and forest. There is nothing prettier to see than the forest and the sun just when the fog is lifting. However, with the crossing of Chamberlain to Lock Dam we were told it might get nasty again. That, no one wanted.

Tents and gear were reloaded again. By the time we had eaten breakfast, it was clearing and gave the appearance of a beautiful day. The lake was calm, and as we glided along we talked back and forth of what Chamberlain Lake was like many years ago. For this was where the last of the river drives, the last of the steam log haulers, and the last of private logging railroads were seen.

We had seen mountains of pulp in the days of Edouard Lacroix. It set us wondering if ever this forest would become as rich in lumber as it was then. After a few years cuttings since the Lacroix operation some thirty years ago, we find the trees are so closely grown together that hardly a deer can go through. The entire Allagash wilderness country resembles a brush pile instead of a forest.

From the air, it looks very nice and inviting. However, once on foot, you must follow roads in order to get to your destination. The old woodsmen say that once a man could walk all day in the forest and not take his ax off his shoulder the entire trip. Today one must crawl, go over downfall, and work in a very difficult manner to get out.

All good things come to an end, so we realized that one cannot keep a forest intact, and that modern equipment and push-button mills must operate with a greater amount of lumber, and time must change, as we change in years.

We arrived at Lock Dam in the early part of the day. There again at this point, we unloaded the gear and carried it over the dam. We asked the damkeeper to give us some water in order to float the canoes down to the headwaters of Eagle Lake, though the carry is only a few rods. This is done by opening a pipe to let the water through underneath the dam.

As you see the water rising on the other side of the carry, one can tell pretty well just how long it must run. Most always the keeper does not give much water, and the guides have to drag the canoes through it. The distance is a mile. If wishes and curses would have anything to do with bad luck and misfortune, the Hydro-Electric Company of Bangor would have failed many years ago, since it is in their honor that the water in Chamberlain Lake had been reversed to run down the Penobscot River.

Needless to say, that part of the Allagash trip is not the most enjoyable. However, it seems that most people adapt themselves to this amount of hardship, and make the trip in spite of it all.

We can say we were most fortunate this day. The ladies and I talked the caretaker blind, treated him with candy bars, asked a million questions, while during this time the water of Chamberlain was raising the waterway higher every minute in the headwaters of Eagle Lake. Soon we had ample, and as the guides drifted easily, saying we have never had it so good, we women walked the old tote road to the final landing where we could see Eagle Lake.

Strawberries were plentiful, and enough were picked for a light lunch. At this point the bank is elevated so that we could see the entire head of the lake. While looking through my field glasses I spotted a moose in the far back grassy point on our left. I was able to holler to Dave and the Old Guide about it.

At once our idea was to try to get close enough to him to take pictures. They picked us up at the usual place and we drifted silently and slowly to where we could see the moose. It was busy feeding, and did not notice our intruding.

When we got closer, we learned it was a cow moose of about two years old. The Old Guide gave a little sound through his lips, similar to a young moose calling its mother. She raised her head and looked directly at him, never taking her eyes off him. The ladies were breathless at the sight and of being so close to a wild animal. I said gently and low, to the Old Guide, "She's a lady; she likes you." He rocked the canoe and said, "Shh, don't say a word." We watched the animal for a good half-hour, getting closer and closer with each dip of the paddle.

However, seeing that we were now too close for comfort, she slowly turned around and made for the forest.

The run into Eagle Lake and across it was mirror-like. The ladies paddled right along as if they were paid to, except to them it was sheer enjoyment. They were strong, rugged, and were not afraid to share the work around the camp.

The guide decided that we would make camp at Ziggler camping ground, saying we had gone far enough for one day. Ziggler campground is a beautiful one. We spent two days and two nights at Ziggler. There are several large tables and a shelter over the fireplace. It is surrounded with pine and huge spruce. We took advantage of it to clean up and wash a few things. I baked a molasses cake, a johnnycake, and more biscuits. I made a fruit salad, and since the strawberries were plentiful, we had strawberry shortcake, and saved enough for the following day to eat with a fruit salad.

On the second night there it rained very hard and the ladies got wet during the night; most of their clothing was dampened by the rainstorm coming in through the little window of their tent which they failed to close when the storm started.

So the following morning everything was hung up by the fireplace to dry, while we packed the gear and loaded the canoes. It all finally dried up. We had had a wonderful day.

The run-through to Churchill was smooth again. So far, we had not stopped to visit any of the landmarks along the lakes, such as the Tramway, the old Camp Parson's place, and the other historical places that I had once enjoyed visiting with my husband. A ten-day trip on the Allagash is soon used up. And all one can do is keep floating slowly and enjoying the scenery and camping.

Arriving at Churchill Lake our minds drifted to Chase Carry, which is ten miles of fast-running water. I had been promised that I did not have to go through, for I do not like fast water, especially with a loaded canoe and three persons in it. Therefore, we waited at the head of Chase Carry for someone to ferry our gear around. Luckily we met someone who was willing to take us along.

I came around with the gear, and the ladies went on down. Needless to say, I was happy to be riding instead of coming down Chase Carry.

In the company of the forest ranger's wife at Umsaskis Lake I waited for my party to arrive. However, before I realized it, I found myself walking down the shore to a secluded spot. I wanted to daydream.

Some thirty-two years before, I had come to this very lake as a young bride. I could not see our little cabin in the cove; nevertheless, it was there in my mind as clear as day when I looked in that direction. What a haven that was for a honeymoon, as well as a wonderful place to bring up three babies.

My eyes drifted to the ledge where I used to go fishing, then on up the other shore to the Pacquets' and the Tarrs'.

There was no sign of there ever being a cabin built, over there. In thirty-two years the forest changes. The only thing left were the two huge pine trees that stood back across the lake a few miles up on a ridge. They were still standing like sentinels, looking over the entire Allagash region; only now they were so very old that only bare branches remained. Oh, how time passes! It was as if I was reading a book, a wonderful book of our life, except at one part a dark cloud appeared, which shaded our life together, and gave us grief and sorrow. Otherwise our book would have had a happy ending.

While this dark cloud hung over our heads, it was in this part of the Maine woods that we sought refuge, to find ourselves again; here we could think, remember, and learn to accept God's wishes.

The sound of an outboard brought me back to reality, and I hurried to the wharf to meet them. Again the canoes were reloaded, and the Old Guide announced that we would stay at Long Lake dam overnight.

The trip across Umsaskis is five miles. The lake was calm and all went well. Soon we arrived in view of Long Lake. Chemquassabamticook stream appeared on our left, followed by the Old Harvey Farm. There were still signs of a field and the place where the old house had stood.

Long Lake Dam—which had once held water from Eagle Lake, Churchill Lake, and Umsaskis Lake—was dilapidated, and very little part of it was left. We carried up over the bank, and began to make a camp for the night.

I pan-fried trout which the others had caught in Chase Carry during the afternoon; everyone was busy setting up tents. Someone said, "There is a storm coming." Then someone would laugh, saying we'd better hurry then. The table was set, and all the goodies on it, and covered with the plastic cloth. I called, "Soup's on-n-n." Everyone was too busy to hear my call. The wind was then blowing, stronger than a breeze. I called a third time, "Come and get it—it's beginning to rain!"

We had no more than helped ourselves to trout, mashed potatoes, and creamed peas when the rain began to fall in torrents. The only tent available to get into was our own tent, which is a Baker-style. It is as old as the hills. If you so much as touch it with your little finger, it begins to leak. With the five of us in a seven-by-seven tent, we might just as well have stayed out in the rain, for in just a few minutes water was beating through. Rain floated our food on our plates and my supper was ruined.

The storm lasted two hours, everyone was wet to the bone, and we shivered ourselves warm. After the storm the guides hurried to make a piping-hot fire, and the process of drying out clothes began; a new meal got in the making, and so went a new experience for Mrs. Brown and Mrs. Doctor.

We looked forward to Round Pond, which is ten miles below, for there we could get under cover. The Old Guide has a beautiful set of sporting camps in Round Pond. We would stay two days there; time to rest, wash, clean up, and especially, to dry our clothes.

It was like being in the best of hotels. Soon the two days were over, and it was time to head down the river again.

A fifteen-mile drift was ahead of us, but everyone felt fresh again and rested. We fished, stopped for tea, and did a lot of discussing about the riverway and all it stood for.